The Essence

of the

Everlasting Phoenix

By

J. J. Mack

Ladybyrd
Publishing

The Essence of the Everlasting Phoenix/by J.J. Mack

© 2013 by J.J. Mack

© 2013 cover art The Everlasting Phoenix/by Lucas Thon

Published by Ladybyrd Publishing

Edited by Drollene P. Brown

Cover Design by Lucas Thon

Typesetting and interior design by Scot Cary

Printed by Xerographic Copy Center, Gainesville FL

Printed in the United States of America

ISBN: 978-0-9898099-1-7
Library of Congress Number Pending
Price: $9.99

Cataloging-in-Publication Data

J.J. Mack 1971-
The Essence of the Everlasting Phoenix/by J.J. Mack

.

ISBN: 978-0-9898099-1-7
1. J.J. Mack 1971- 2. Spirituality. 3. Inspiration.
4. Separateness. 5. Oneness. 6. Acceptance. 7. Advaita.
8. Vedanta. 9. Non-dualism.

                        I. Title
                        CIP

10 9 8 7 6 5 4 3 2 1

This
Book
Is
Dedicated
To
My
Three Wise Men,
Kenny, Bernard and Paul

Contents

Acknowledgments

I should like to acknowledge the following people:

My parents, Maureen and Jim.

Jill, Jackie and Garry.

Lucas for his awesome cover art.

Drollene Brown for her patience with my terrible spelling,

Pamela Raines for believing in me and helping me become self-employed.

And also all my other family and friends for their love, patience and encouragement.

Special thanks to Dr. Kenneth Leeb for his guidance and unconditional love, support and never-ending knowledge.

Translated Sayings

Absolute + Consciousness + The body (Hindu Tradition)

Father + Holy Spirit + The Son

Father = Sperm = Seed = Source

Apocalypse—An unveiling

Bathos—Divine depth

Buddha—The enlightened one

Christ—The anointed one

Ego—Separate entity from God, with free will and control

Ginza—Treasure

Gnosis—Knowledge; wisdom

Heaven, Kingdom of—Revelation, all is God

Hell—Separate from God

Islam—Surrender to God

Isloga—Surrender to the already present union with God

Karma—1. Action your life takes. 2. Action your life takes without your opinion on whether that action is good or bad.

Sin—To miss the mark, the mark being the Idea that you are separate from God. All other usage of the word sin is then from the mind of man using it to mean good or bad, which is also a man-made idea, for good and bad do not exist in the eyes of God, but only in the opinions of mankind.

Soul (in Greek)—Psyche

Yoga—Union with God

Introduction

For the first 33 years of my life I lived just like anyone else. I had a sense of separateness and saw myself as an individual who was separate from the universe, separate from other people, but most of all, separate from God. I was born and I would die. Of this I was sure. Born in Ronkonkoma, Long Island, New York, I was raised Catholic. I was told as a little boy that God was somewhere "up there" and the devil was somewhere "down there." As far back as I can remember I didn't buy it.

In the Catholic religion you don't receive Communion until the age of seven. For Communion you wait in line near the end of the hour-long Mass to receive a wafer-like cracker that represents the body of Christ. One morning in church with my family I asked my father, "What am I supposed to do?"

He whispered that I should walk up to the altar, the priest would say, "The body of Christ," then I would say, "Amen." Then when I walked back to my seat I was supposed to have "a good feeling inside."

The only good feeling I ever had was knowing after I received Communion there was only about ten minutes left to the Mass and I could get out of there and we could all go back home. I did not like it. As a matter of fact as a very little boy it scared me. When I walked through the doors of the church, directly in front of me, hanging above the altar was a horrific-looking dead man, twice the size of a regular man, nailed to a cross. What an image for a five-year-old boy to see! It gave me nightmares. I didn't understand it. As a young boy I was very inquisitive. I asked many questions about God to many, many people. And would you believe it, I got a different answer almost every time. I could feel shreds of truth sometimes, but most of the time it felt fake. It felt as if people were just making it up as they went along, and what's really strange is that it didn't feel as though they were lying. They actually believed what they were saying as they answered me even though it might have been the first time they ever said it.

When I got older and my questions got deeper, the answer became "just have faith" and "give the church 10% of your salary for the rest of your life." Once again: not buying it!

Both my parents went to Catholic High School in the early '60s—my father in Brooklyn and my mother in the Bronx. They got married in May 1970 and moved out to Long Island. I was born in June 1971, and although they wanted to put me in Catholic School, they couldn't afford it, so public school it was. Consequently after a full week of public school in grades one through six, I went to religion classes on Saturdays. To put it mildly, it sucked. When I was in the fifth grade one Saturday morning, the teacher was telling us about Noah's ark. I raised my hand and questioned her. "How is that possible? Aren't there thousands of different types of spiders alone?" I asked. "How could he have gotten two of every living creature on earth in a boat all at once in a short period of time?"

The teacher seemed stunned and barked back at me, obviously feeling embarrassed by my question. "There were fewer animals around at that time."

That didn't seem like the correct answer to me. Once again it felt as though she were making it up. Once again I wasn't buying it.

~

As I entered my teenage years I was overweight, very shy and more confused about God than ever. My idea of God, like that of everyone else I knew, was that God was some person-like being that had all the regular attributes of a human being. I heard things like "God is angry," "God is sad," "God is unhappy," God is this, and God is that. This is where my troubles with God really started to increase. If God was a person-like, separate entity with logic and reasoning, how could "He" allow all these terrible things to happen to innocent people? He was always talked about as a father. It wasn't until I was much older that I realized when Jesus said the word father he was referring to what a father produces: sperm. And what is sperm? It is a seed. And what is a seed? It is the source. So father = sperm = seed = source. The source of all things. I will elaborate later in the book.

I would pray to God for help, but I never saw it come. So I started to grow angrier until finally I started to hate this God I was hearing so much about. It made no sense at all to me. Some of the questions I had were:

How could God feel unhappy? "He" was God, after all. Couldn't he just make himself happy?

Why did it seem that humans were the center of the universe? The universe is an awfully big place, and all God seemed concerned with was this tiny little planet, with at the time back in 1986 only had four billion people on it. Didn't "He" have other stuff to do?

I couldn't figure it out. Unless ... unless the entire idea of God being a separate entity was incorrect. With the idea of God being a daddy, nothing seemed to fit. But if it was all wrong, God being a person, God having human attributes, God being a creator, all of it, then at least it left the door open for some other explanation.

What that explanation was I hadn't the slightest idea. It seemed to me insane that God was a person watching our every move. What a paranoid existence that would be! And it sure was. Those teenage years, 13-18 were filled with anger, loneliness, fear and hatred. Those ingredients were mixing together, and by 18 I was ready to explode. I had denounced any affiliation with the Catholic Church. I had suffered immeasurably as a child, both physically and mentally. I had been in the emergency room six times in 18 years for stitches on different parts of my body. I was teased and picked on terribly by other kids. I had no voice to fight back because of the oppression I suffered as a child. I was miserable, and I blamed God for everything. How could "He" let this happen? Unless ...

~

In addition to normal desires as I entered into adulthood, I had many, many fears and feelings of anxiety, resentment, anger and aggression. I harbored thoughts of suicide, revenge and hatred. My life was in a constant state of flux. I would, for a very short time, become high on life, and then I would crash back down into depression and sadness. I tried every conceivable way to alleviate my pain and almost constant, unbearable suffering, bouncing back and forth from drug use to sex to food. I shopped around, trying out new religions, knowing that although it was quite obvious to me that organized, dogmatic religions didn't work, underneath the fear and the shame and the guilt, there might be a shred of truth. I slowly came to believe that "life-long faith" is the last refuge for the shallow spiritual teacher. I could never find peace in a religion that uses fear, shame, guilt and threats on the one hand and on the other tells you just to have faith for your whole life and "know we love you." It is a psychotic and sad quagmire of unhealthiness, oppression and abuse.

It was through this painful existence and the questioning and investigating of all these belief structures that the truth was revealed to me. Never did I allow myself the conformity of naiveté or to just "have faith" when I asked a question of different people and got different answers! In which answer was I supposed to have faith?

In the early part of the 21st century, one night before going to bed I was reading a book titled *Net of Jewels*, by Ramesh Balsakar, a well known and loved sage from India. The next morning when I awoke, I suddenly knew something, all on its own, had changed. I was awake and alive and aware, but there was no thought going through my mind. It was the most beautiful silence I have ever heard! This silence continued for about ten minutes as I sat, frozen. As the thought flow returned, I knew I was not who I had thought I was for all those years. My entire identity had been temporarily erased. How could I be this separate entity when my very identity had vanished? Who was I? What was I? At that point I started to realize I was not this body nor was I this mind. Then through meditation and self inquiry I started to associate "myself" as a witnessing presence, which at this point was still an identity, but a much different one than had ever been there before.

Life suddenly had drastically changed for me. There was an incredible release of feelings and energy that had been bottled up for so long. I had a strange peace about me that had never been there before—a kind of ease and gentleness. So, like any good, spiritual seeker, I started to investigate everything I could get my hands on. I read as many books as I possibly could on a daily basis. I was intoxicated—possessed you might say. Nothing was going to stop me from finding out who I really was. I read books by Ramana Maharshi, Nisargadatta Maharaj (my favorite), Eckhart Tolle and Ramesh Balsakar; and poems by Rumi and Maria Rilke. In addition I read the Gita and the Tao Te Ching. I just kept reading and reading and reading.

Over the next few months, as the understanding deepened, it was through the negative reactions of other people that I started to realize the depth of what had happened. Although I feverishly tried to explain my experiences, what was transpiring within me was beyond words, and the reaction from people was less than enthusiastic. The relationship with my girlfriend dissolved. People I considered good friends no longer remained close to me. My family thought I had gone completely insane. Some people got so angry when I spoke about it they told me they never wanted to talk about it again. Most people just looked at me with a dazed look in their eyes. Had I gone totally mad? Were people correct when they told me I was crazy?

Suddenly and completely spontaneously, a friend and mentor revealed to me that he, too, had had this experience 30 years earlier. At that point the way I had been viewing him changed. I became his disciple, and he became my Guru.

I

You Have Always Been Naked

1
God Just Is

I can't tell you anything about God
Because there's nothing to tell.
God has no attributes.
God just *is*.

In some of the poems and essays written in this book it appears as though I'm speaking of God as a separate entity.

God is not a separate entity.

This is just a way of saying there has been a surrender of any idea that there is a me here, in control with free will.

We can point to God using parables or words such as "God is like ..." as in God is like the gears inside a clock. The gears inside a clock are "in control" or are "in charge" of making the clock work correctly. Yet they are not making a choice or conscious decision about the functioning of the clock. Nor do they care what time it is. This is what God is like.

2
Surrender
(#1)

Dear Lord,

All is yours from every grain of sand to every snowflake to every piece of salt in your mighty oceans. I am not worthy of your greatness, nor of your gifts— legs with which to walk so that I need not slither on the ground, fingers with which to touch and eyes with which to see. These gifts are too great for me. Take them back if it is thy will, and I shall still be overjoyed with what you have let me keep.

You have given me more than I deserve and allowed me to be humble and thankful. Dare I presume that humility and thankfulness are your greatest gifts, for what more do I need? If you have graced me with thankfulness, nothing else matters, for I can now be thankful for anything and everything that comes my way regardless of what other people may think I should be thankful for.

I am reborn into the void and have been extinguished by you. Nothing there is that I should call my own. Even my blood, which you have graciously lent me; even my beating heart, which started beating from stillness with no doing of my own—take them from me or continue to let the blood flow and the heart to beat, for I will not utter a word either way.

My bones and flesh belong to you; how clever, one being hard and the other supple. Yet you are too great to even worship, for who am I to have that privilege?

Use me until I am used up, no matter the place or time of my expiration. What a wonder it is you allow my lungs to fill with air, for even this I am not worthy. Nor am I worthy of writing these words, for it is your hand that guides mine as such it should be. Even my complete and total surrender to you is you, for I am less than empty space. Needs, I have none. For the wants I have, ashamed am I.

I want to heal the sick. feed the hungry and poor and give my blood and organs to those who have need of them. Disassemble me and hand me out to the ones you choose, for even of this presence that is everywhere, I am still not worthy.

The Essence of the Everlasting Phoenix

3
To Thine Own Self Be True

When the new spring is upon us
We are filled with hope and joy anew.
We feel that our dreams will be answered
As we step outside to see morning's dew.

But do we need to feel morning's security
In order to be reborn?
Or should we look deep inside ourselves
To repair what has been torn?

The need for love is all around us
As the world heats up and starts to cook
Confusion and turmoil seem everywhere,
But we must take a deeper look.

We should not judge and hate each other
As so many people often do
For all the pain and suffering that is
Begins with the hate inside you.

For if we truly love ourselves,
Love that starts at our core,
All the Rage and the Violence,
The Suffering, would be no more.

Niruta

4
You Have Always
Been Naked

Obviously you know when you are naked, but aren't you always naked under your clothes? Now, let's say you put on another layer of clothing. Even though you are still completely naked, you start to "lose sight" of your nakedness until, eventually, after thousands and thousands of layers of clothing are put on, you completely forget about your nakedness. You have *always* been naked. You always will be naked. Although there may be a subtle "knowing" of nakedness, you have lost your conviction. Since you have "forgotten" you are naked, you look outward for your very nakedness!

One day out of the blue, someone tells you that you are actually nakedness itself. At this point, after decades of piling on hundreds of thousands of layers of clothing, you are told that you are what you're looking for. So you start to ask yourself, am I really naked? How will I know? Soon you realize that finding out whether you're naked is about removing, not gaining, anew. You start to remove layers of clothing. Sometimes one hundred layers at a time. As more and more layers fall away, it almost seems as if it's happening on its own, without there being a doer.

You can now practically feel your nakedness. It seems to be getting closer, or *is it just that everything seems to be falling off of me*? As the deepest layers of clothing evaporate, it becomes almost painful and maddening, then spontaneously the first layer disintegrates and there you are in your glorious nakedness *I am naked*! I've always been naked! And a smile appears upon your face as you walk across the room to close the blinds.

5
The Three Levels
(Yet There Are No Levels)

Many people are completely stuck in illusion. As I see it, there are three levels of spirituality, with level one having the angriest people, the ones needing the most love and forgiveness. This is a level of spirituality because we all have the potential in us to become sons and daughters of God. Level two has the majority of humans. Level three is made up of those who experience oneness with God.

Level One

Those in Level One are angry, hateful and bitter, always blaming God or someone else for their problems, rarely taking responsibility for any of their actions, always looking for some scapegoat. They are the ones who seem to have no conscience at all. Not only are they stuck to a "me" who seems to be in charge, they are very rarely compassionate. They see forgiveness as a weakness, and love seems to be absent from their lives. They are the ones who commit genocide with a smile, totally enmeshed in egoic delusion. They are the haters, supremacists and ultimate control freaks. I suppose many of them have never known love, so there is no love to give away. Many of them have been hurt in terribly grisly ways as children and have grown up to become worse than their oppressors. With that being said, it is never too late for grace.

A prime example is the author of the song "Amazing Grace." It was written by the captain of a slave-trading ship. This man fits perfectly into level one of spirituality. By most standards we would say this slave ship captain was an awful human being, a miserable wretch. He traded human lives for money. Just think of the three- or four-month journey from the west coast of Africa to the Americas. A quarter of them never made it across the Atlantic, thrown overboard when they died in their shackles. Those who lived endured beatings, rapes, sea-sickness and hunger, but the worst may have been knowing they had been sold into slavery by other African tribes and that they were to be sold again in the Americas, never to be free again.

Jesus said, "God makes his sun to rise on the evil and on the good, and sends rain on the just and on the unjust" (Matthew 5: 45). There was no benevolent will that led the captain to find grace; grace came upon him. No matter where you are in life, and no matter what you have done in your past or have had done to you, there is always the chance for grace.

First you must forgive yourself. You are your worst enemy. Shame and guilt will block you from knowing the grace of God. They are huge obstacles on the path to enlightenment. It took a long time for guilt and shame to build up in you, and although it will take a little time for them to go, they will leave much quicker than it took for them to build up. Once again it is different for each person, but with constant awareness and continual forgiving of yourself they should be absent in one or two to three years, with huge chunks falling away at a time. When I say gone, I mean it as totally, completely and unequivocally gone. Imagine a life with no guilt or shame. It is guilt and shame that perpetuates those actions over and over again. When I have said this in the past to people, sometimes their response has been that without guilt or shame you will have a license to do anything bad you want to do to people. This is not true, and here is why: it is all God. Every thought, every action is God. When this deep, profound insight hits, it tends to alleviate your wrong doings.

There is a newfound lightness about you, and with it comes a deep caring for everyone and everything.

You have a happiness that is felt in every one of your hundred trillion cells. Your once-believed "choice" is no longer there, replaced with a feeling of such immense gratitude, you are compelled to be of service to all God's extensions. I say extensions because everything is literally God. At this point revenge is replaced with forgiveness, anger with love, and shame and guilt with gratitude and service. Okay, so now the shame and guilt are gone. That wasn't so bad, was it?

Next is a word you have heard many times. It can have many definitions, but the definition I will use for this word is unconditional. You guessed it; the word is love. The word love in this manifested universe has an opposite; let's call it hate. I love you, unless I catch you cheating on me, and then that love quickly turns to hate. What does this tell us? Love-hate are the distant ends of interconnective opposites, which means they are like one word, used in reference to the circumstances of whatever situation is happening in your life. This is why I'm defining love as unconditional. Love that has no conditions and is not dependent on external circumstances. It is beyond *deep*. It is the purest feeling we can have in manifestation.

You must have unconditional love for yourself, regardless of your past. Practice by looking in a mirror and telling yourself you unconditionally love yourself and know you are worthy of that unconditional love. Tell yourself you unconditionally love yourself while you drive your car, take a shower or cook a meal. Say it so much and so often to the point you think you can't possibly say it again, then double your efforts. Look at it as though there is a reservoir inside you that becomes filled with love and cannot overflow because the more you love yourself the bigger the actual container grows and keeps growing. Then you can take from that reservoir, this unconditional love, and give it freely to the world, always continually adding to it inside yourself. It can never be filled, for the world is always in need of love.

But before you can give it away you must have some, so practice, practice, practice, until it is no longer a practice.

Level Two

The second level is the one into which the majority of people fit. Many people around the globe have been starting to wake up from the dream of being an individual doer, although it is a rare case for full realization. The reason for this is that for a full realization to happen there must be total and complete surrender to God of any trace of identity. Within or without what I call the second level of spirituality, there are many different sub-levels. There are some who, for the first time after spending their lives in complete illusion, just get a glimpse of the totality of everything. Out of nowhere—maybe sitting at the beach, or involved in a painful event—something just switches in their minds as if it is flooded with light, and they suddenly know they are not who they thought they were all along. This is not full realization, but it is the beginning of a movement into the oneness that has always been there, waiting. And so their journey begins, possibly with a relentlessness that is unstoppable.

I have seen many people who have had this first glimpse suddenly stop short along the path as if their feet were embedded in concrete. It seems that when people who were suffering mildly have this beginning awakening, it brings them up to a certain place along the path, bringing some relief and a little peace into their lives, there they stay. I've seen it again and again.

It takes every drop of courage you have to continue, and people are afraid of the unknown. But fear not, for as you continue, the courage is there waiting for you, and inside you there is more courage than you could ever possibly imagine. You must continue to push through the fear, the loneliness, the painful memories and so on. Ah, but the ego is a tricky one and will come up with thousands and thousands of reasons for you to give up, all because it believes itself to be in charge, in control, and having free will. So it, the ego, or sense of separate doership will morph and change and do anything to survive. Yet it is not real in the first place!

The same way a tiger chasing you in a dream while you are in bed sleeping is not real, that's the way the ego is not real. Although that tiger may seem very, very real as it chases you in your dream, once you wake up from that dream it is all over, and you are safe in your bed. So was the tiger real? Your belief made it appear real, but once you awoke from the dream, you no longer *believed* the tiger was real and so it no longer had any effect on you. It is the exact same way with the ego. It is a *belief* that there is a *you* separate from God that makes you appear real, but once the dream is over the ego no longer has any effect except for an occasional residue of memory.

On another sub-level in Level Two, there are people who have progressed, so to speak, on the spiritual path. They have practiced forgiveness. They may be very kind and loving. They may have a deep, profound understanding of oneness, but as I said previously, the ego is a tricky one, and this is where the ego, in order to survive, will settle down, stop causing trouble and take on a very spiritual identity. Yet it is an identity nonetheless, and this is still where only a few people get: right at the edge of nothingness, but still consciousness holds on. A dream is a dream, no matter how advanced the illusory ego may have gotten, no matter how much it acts spiritual, it is still lost in a dream, albeit a nicer dream. As long as the beliefs of doership, freewill and control are there, no matter how nice they appear to have become, this is not full realization.

Level Three

The third level of full realization is the rarest of the rare, although available to anyone, male or female. The fully realized "person"—for lack of a better term—knows no bounds and has no rules. Humans on this level are truly free to play any part they wish in this play called life, even if it sometimes seems contradictory to the seeker. Many unrealized teachers, whether on purpose or because of their own ignorance tell their students to follow all kinds of rules to reach enlightenment. A true Guru takes away; he does not give the student things. This is why seekers *Guru-shop* from teacher to teacher until they find one who tells them what they want to hear. Many Gurus and seekers disagree with me because their egos do not want to hear it, and they want rules to follow. Although at times some of these things may be helpful to the seekers or to anyone for that matter, they are not imperative for enlightenment. Here are a few things that do *not* have to happen for realization to occur:

- You do not have to stop eating meat and become a vegetarian.
- You do not have to stop smoking cigarettes ... or give up pot, for that matter.
- You do not have to stop having sex.

One funny think I heard: a spiritual teacher named Eckart Tolle said once when people recognized him when he was drinking coffee exclaimed that he shouldn't be drinking coffee because he was a spiritual teacher. He solved the problem by wearing a baseball cap when he goes to Starbucks.

The man who started the Krishna sect of Hinduism told his students, among other things, they couldn't even eat eggs! So let me see if I have this correct: my true nature is the unmanifested source or potentiality of everything manifest, but I can't have an Egg McMuffin? Many teachers have become very wealthy telling people what they can and can't do. The ego loves rules, paths and goals. If there is something you can or cannot do, there must still be the idea of a "you" there to do it. Yet there is no "you"; there never has been, never will be. That is why the enlightened sage is free to do whatever life brings to him/her, fitting into any situation that there is at any given time. When we hear the words of the Guru we naturally only take them in conceptually. But then after hearing the words we are transformed, and we transcend those words, no longer having any use for them.

There is a dangerous place along the spiritual path. It comes after there is some depth of understanding; the ego or sense of being a separate entity doer, still seen as being real, grabs onto those words and inflates itself being a more spiritual person than someone else. This has a way of locking the consciousness deeper into illusion. People are so very used to the idea of understanding things conceptually, and it is rare for the consciousness to let go of the idea it is a person, turn in on itself and then transcend all concepts and ideas.

Remember you are not giving up your free will, for you never had any free will; there never has been a you there to have it. What is surrendered is the *idea* of there being a *me* there with free will. You don't lose your free will; it is just now seen to have never existed before in the first place. There must be full, total and complete surrender of any idea of your being in charge of anything. The sooner this is done, the quicker it will take for the realization that all there is, is God, and the sooner you will become a servant to mankind. Then a bliss is in and around you always and can never be taken away by anyone or anything. This is why Christ, dying and in pain, nailed to the cross, said, "Forgive them for they know not what they do." If I had to break it down to three things on which all level-three masters would agree, they would be these:

1. Everything is God.

2. Heaven, hell and rebirth are stories for the unenlightened.

3. Free will is a trick the mind plays on consciousness.

6
Explanation of Pointers

You will hear me say again and again that words fail us when we are speaking about that which cannot be put into words or understood with the mind, or intellect. So I like to use the word *pointer* to let you know whether I am using the word only pointing to the truth, not actually describing it. It is a mere signpost, guiding you in the direction of truth. Many teachers will use the same words to mean different things, all of them possibly correct, so it is important to learn the style of whatever teacher you may be listening to or reading. For this book I shall try to differentiate certain terms or words I use to point to that which is unnamable; all the words below point to that no-thing that is prior to manifestation but yet not a *thing* at all.

Source
Pure Awareness
Unmanifested
Potential
The Unnamable
That
The Unknowable
The Absolute
God
The Father

All these words point to the same no-thing that is the source of everything.

7
The Switch

Jesus was quoted as saying, "I am the light of the world; he who follows me shall not walk in darkness, but shall have the light of life" (John 8:12). As I have said before, sometimes Jesus spoke from the point of view of the person Jesus, at other times from the point of view of the source and still at other times from the POV of the Holy Spirit, giving it a completely different identity and voice.

In the statement above he is switching his point of view from a person and speaking from the source, as if it had a voice. This is very tricky, but if you look for it you will see him switch back and forth talking from the POV of a person as in Luke 23:34, while hanging on the cross dying, he said of the soldiers who crucified him, "Father, forgive them for they know not what they do."

When he said, "Before Abraham was, I am," he once again switches and speaks from the manifested I am. This "I" will be seen as the light of existence or consciousness or the manifested "I am." This can sometimes be a common practice with the realized person, as in lord Krishna's statement from the Bhagavad Giga in verse 10:20: "I am the beginning and the life span of beings, and there end as well."

Krishna did not mean his person or his body is the beginning and the end, just as Jesus didn't mean that Jesus the person was born or existed before the person Abraham existed. The point of view in both cases is the manifested I am. From that POV, then yes, before Abraham was, "I, the consciousness am."

In John 14:11 Jesus, who is speaking to Philip says, "Believe me when I say that I am in the father and the father is in me." This is now showing Jesus talking from the unmanifested source or potential to be, by passing, so to speak, the manifested I am, and from person to source and source to person.

In John 12:46 Jesus says, "I have come into the world as light, so that everyone who believes in me should not remain in darkness." In the first part of the saying Jesus uses the words "I" and "light." Now from only the seeker's POV, this will be understood as though Jesus means his body or person. When the understanding has deepened, however, this "I" will be seen as the light of existence, or consciousness, or the manifested I am. In the second part he says the word "me." Once again this could be seen as his person, or if the understanding has expanded, so to speak, or it will be a statement from the "I am."

This is why religion can be so confusing, because if you don't know about this switch of perception, so to speak, then it looks or seems as if Jesus is saying everything from just his point of view, which he is not, and can then be terribly misunderstood.

Another famous quote by Jesus is when he answered a question from one of his disciples, Thomas, by saying "I am the way and the truth and the life" (John 14:6). He did not mean that he, Jesus is the life, but that "I," the big I, or the source, if it could speak, would say, "I am the way, the truth and the life." Once you begin to look for and see this "switch," everything becomes much clearer and you start to understand on a much deeper level. So now with this newfound knowledge go back to your Bible or Gita or other spiritual books and look for the "switch," and you'll find it over and over again, making it easier to understand.

What I have just written is something I never see discussed, although I believe it is a major key in deciphering or getting a handle on how spiritual teachers speak and look at things. Once realization happens, teachers never seem to point out this very important piece of the puzzle—maybe because they see everything as one anyhow, and don't feel it is necessary to explain. But I believe that it is an invaluable part of the teaching. So look for it in what you are reading and you will suddenly see it popping out all over the place.

Another wonderful example of Jesus' using "the switch" is in the Gospel of Thomas, saying #77. You will find a further explanation of this in "The (Coptic) Gospel of Thomas," Chapter 25.

8
Things I Have Learned
(#1)

- "Judging" can cause pain, suffering anger, hate, resentment, revenge, violence, fear and death.

- Being compassionate helps you as much as it helps the other person.

- Acceptance is the key to lasting happiness.

- The only cure to mankind's biggest problem (which is fear) is unconditional love.

- The more you investigate life the less you fear it.

- Awareness of a problem is how you overcome it.

- The answer one hundred percent of the time is, "No, you don't look fat in that!"

9
Fall From Grace

There I am, alone in my darkness, peace. Suddenly, and as quietly as a nighttime snowfall, a powerful presence is upon me. Space is everywhere. I am light. I am presence. I am everything everywhere, and everything is me.

I <u>AM</u> that.
☋ Tribute to nisargadatta☋

Why do you have to be told you're a person? If it were true wouldn't you know it right from the start? Why did it take about three years to be convinced that you're a person? A deeper question is "Who is it that's been convinced?

10
I Am/I Am Not

I am the Beginningless Circle,
I am the Void, yet filled to the brim.
I am everywhere Immensely, Infinite,
I am Totality and before ...

I am the Light of the World.
I am free, for the Universe depends
    on me.
I am hidden, yet you can find me in
    the spaciousness, for there is no
    place I am not.

I am a vast Ocean of Awareness prior
    to Time and Space.
Beginningless, Endless, Immovable,
    Uncaused, no Shape, no Form,
    no Identity.

11
Karma

If you are sure of the immediate, you will never reach the ultimate. So ... what are you *sure* of? The realized sage knows the only thing you can be sure of is that everything is God. Unfortunately we are in short supply of fully realized masters, especially in the west. Your everyday person seems so sure of so many things, but on the spiritual path, everything—and I mean *everything* in the broadest sense of the word—must be questioned.

The things that should be questioned and investigated repeatedly are some of the most basic things that are taken for granted: Am I really just a person? Have I been born? Am I in the universe or is the universe in me? Do I have parents? Do I have children? Do I have a name? On one level, the level of the dream world—or as the Hindus call it MAYA—these things may seem true, but what is truth anyway? I am speaking of the deepest truth there is, not the truths of the everyday imaginary dream world of choice, control and free will.

Years ago I asked my teacher, "Are there different levels of understanding?"

His answered brilliantly, saying, "There are levels, but there are no levels."

I gave him a strange look, because he never seemed to give me a straight answer. The ego wants answers; it wants something concrete to sink its teeth and claws into, and my teacher knew this. Far ahead of me, he never gave me anything to hold onto, and for this I thank him from the bottom of my heart. The mind wants information and rules and systems and linear paths to achieve something at the end of a teaching. With this spiritual teaching, the exact opposite happens.

If you went to a weekend workshop on spirituality that costs, let's say $500, you are going to want to "learn" a bunch of stuff you can take home with you. You want something that will inflate your ego, something that will keep the seeker further stuck in illusion. If the teacher comes out on Saturday and says, "It's all God," and on Sunday does the same thing, and that's all he says, the people might have a fit, demanding their money back. Moreover, they'll speak badly about the class and teacher to everyone they know. Most students of spirituality want to be told what to do, how long it will take to reach enlightenment and what the benefits "to me" will be. They want to know on what day they can say they are enlightened.

This is nonsense. It is the evaporation of the seeker that leads to the understanding that everything is God. A true spiritual teacher will *take away* from you, not give you anything—*take away* your ideas about God, *take away* your beliefs about after-lifes, *take away* your notions about free will and control. This is why most people follow false messiahs, leading with their egos in order to gain something. Once again I will say that this teaching is about letting go, surrendering to, and questioning your most cherished belief structures, watching them collapse like a building being demolished.

You must see yourself as the space within the building, not the building itself; when the building falls, the space is still there, left intact. That spaciousness is your freedom—freedom from the belief that you were the structure. When the structure is gone, the realization is that you have been the space all along, and it was only an idea or belief that if we do something bad God punishes us. Likewise is the belief that if you do bad karma some bad karma comes back to you. This is just the same old story wearing new clothes. I once knew a hippie who named her dog Karma, and if the dog acted good or bad she would say, "Good Karma," or "Bad Karma." That made me laugh my ass off the first time I heard it.

The new definition of the word Karma should be this: "The action your life takes, without your opinion of whether that action is good or bad." After all, there is no good or bad, just opinions about life events. Also it is our very opinions about life that help to create our false sense of identity, which is probably why the Buddha said, "Have no opinions." Does this mean we should all become mindless robots who never speak about anything? No, of course not.

You can still have an opinion on whether you like vanilla ice cream over chocolate ice cream as long as you accept that if there is no vanilla left you either eat the chocolate or something else and don't complain or identify with not getting vanilla. That kind of behavior is what causes our ghost identity, our unwillingness to bend, keeping us locked in illusion and suffering.

So rejoice and let go, my brothers and sisters, and let come what comes. Let go what goes. Remember it is all God, and the sooner this revelation occurs the sooner this suffering ends, if for just a little while on this earth, and we stop the judging and the hating, the gossip and the violence and build a better world for ourselves, if of course that's how the very random variables "decide" to play out. Now go love someone and have some ice cream.

12
Surrender
(#2)

God,

Thank you for letting me suffer so much and for so long, for it has brought me courage and strength.

Thank you, God, for my loneliness, for it has made me love people more than I could have done on my own.

Thank you, God, for all my physical pain, for it has made me and my touch more tender.

Thank you, God, for all the crazy thoughts in my head, for it has made me understand the thoughts of others better.

Thank you, God, for giving me so much, then taking it away, then giving it back, then taking it away again, because now I can see that none of it is important.

Thank you, God, for making me cry, so that I know how to comfort others who weep.

Thank you, God, for making me sick, so I am able to care for those who are too sick to care for themselves.

Thank you, God, for making me angry, so that I may have compassion for those who show anger toward me.

Thank you, God for letting my heart break, so that I may help mend the hearts of those who need it

Thank you, God, for testing my strength, for it helps me to be more patient.

Thank you, God, for all the joy you have brought me so that I may pass it on to everyone.

But most of all, thank you, God, for all the love you have given me so that I may give it freely to all.

II

What Jesus Really Said

13
Truth is a Matter of Opinion

All we're really doing is comparing perceptions of life with each other.

Your greatest ally and your biggest nemesis is belief.

Belief is what got you into this mess.
Not believing anymore is what can get you out.

Everyone seems to be so interested in what goes on in the universe without ever giving a glance to the Consciousness that makes it all possible.

The best answer to "Who am I?" is "I don't know."

Sub-atomic particles float aimlessly through an Infinite ocean of Emptiness.
We call it life.

14
Illusion

The Organism is completely programmed. This programming (i.e., genes) starts before the sense or feeling of "I Am" arises. The concept "I Am" arises spontaneously because of a chemical reaction that happens in the brain (when the child is two to three years old).

The instinctive knowing "I Am" turns into "I Am Something," and eventually into "I Am a Person." The organism will continue to be programmed throughout its life, the only difference now is the illusory sense of doership. It is this false sense of individual consciousness, this sense of being a completely separate entity, which is the root cause of fear itself and the beginning of all mental suffering. If this "sense of separateness" is investigated, if it is pondered over, brought into the field of awareness, the illusion of personal doership will evaporate the way a flame leaves the wick of a candle when blown out with a breath of fresh air.

Recently, during the period when I was writing this book, I saw an episode of "Through the Wormhole," with Morgan Freeman. On this TV show, a doctor was doing tests on children to show that a child's consciousness grows in stages, so that he is not fully aware of himself until he is five years old. The conclusion was that a person isn't truly alive until this happens.

If there is a belief that there is a "me" here, this would be a good discussion between another illusory "me." Yet from the spiritual POV of Vedanta, it is the other way around. Despite the doctor's conclusion, Vedanta would say the opposite: the consciousness is not growing. When it appears, it is everywhere and everything. Then as the body of the child grows, the manifested consciousness itself starts to shrink, getting smaller and identifying itself, which limits it to just a body. Then after five years, the consciousness, or Holy Spriit, or "I am" sees itself completely as a person with an identity. This is not life, it is death. To be more accurate, it is more like a coma than death.

Then suddenly, when the organism is 30, 40 or 50, a big spiritual explosion may happen, and this is the beginning of the "I am," remembering itself as just consciousness, unadulterated and not attached to name, shape or form. This can be a joyful state, having the consciousness of a two- or three-year old with the brain that is 40. When the "I am" fully recognizes itself, the consciousness would be that of a newborn, still with The workings of a 30-, 40- or 50-year-old mind. This is a very deep state. The disposition of the body will change and probably be happier and more forgiving. Other people will probably see a change in how the body acts. Yet this is still a state. There is that which is prior to the "I am," and although unnamable, it is your true source.

You are both unmanifested and manifested. Although, if you were only manifested, when consciousness turns back into pure awareness, as in deep sleep, after it entered the body again you would not know it had left. It is only because you are simultaneously the changeless awareness behind it, so to speak, that you know it appears and disappears.

15
Ask Yourself

Isn't it just a little bit strange that every sixteen hours or so you and the entire universe just suddenly disappears? And it's gone, and there's no feeling, sensation or even consciousness. Then mysteriously the entire universe, including *you*, reappears with no effort on your part. Isn't that amazing? How can you have free will and control in a world that comes and goes as it pleases?

Who were you on the day you were born?

STAY PUT! All else happens on its own, automatically.

16
What Was Jesus Really Saying?

As we read the Bible over and over, we see how most people got so confused, not understanding the teaching of Jesus. This teaching, which has been around for millennia, has been in every country. Other teachings have come from every nationality: Lao Tsu and Confucius from China; the Buddha, Nisargadatta and Rammana Maharshi from India; William Blake from England; Meister Eckhart from Germany; St. Francis of Assisi from Italy; Kahlil Gibran from Lebanon. In addition to Jesus, other great teachers and philosophers have come from all over the world: Muhammad, Shankara, Pai-chang, Ralph Waldo Emerson, Henry David Thoreau, Abu Sa'id ibn abi'l-Kháyr, Rumi, Rainer Maria Rilke and many others as well. Obviously I have named these in no particular order.

I could spend an hour straight writing down names of people through whom realization has happened, and not even scratch the surface. For even though there have been many, they are still only points of light in an otherwise dark dream world. This is because (and remember words fail us miserably the deeper we go spiritually), once pure awareness manifests into consciousness and then that consciousness hooks into and identifies itself with the body, it sinks its teeth into it, and is then constantly reinforced, all through the life of the person.

Let's say someone at the age of 30 meets a realized person, and the opportunity for enlightenment occurs. Thirty years of entanglement needs to untangle. This is the *dying* about which Jesus was speaking. It is the consciousness that has to let go of everything until finally when there is nothing left with which to identify, it then has to turn in on itself so to speak; at that point it realizes that it is not even consciousness, but the source of consciousness—pure awareness itself. When that last step happens, this is what Jesus refers to as being reborn into the Kingdom of Heaven. This is extremely rare, although totally available to anyone, male or female. A lot of the time, as consciousness starts to wake up and break its identity with the body, it stops; many times this is what people think is enlightenment, which it is not. Even if consciousness has let go of everything but still identifies itself as manifested consciousness, it has not gone all the way home; it stays right there, still lost in identity, even if it is a deep state of understanding.

In "The (Coptic) Gospel of Thomas" (Chapter 25), Jesus speaks about this, saying "If one who knows the all still feels a personal deficiency, he is completely deficient" (#67).

Pure awareness is not an identity. Pure awareness is the absence of consciousness identifying with itself. Only when there is no identity whatsoever is there full realization and complete and total surrender.

John 6:60 reads "Many of his followers said, 'This teaching is too hard. Who can listen to it?'" In the verse that follows Jesus replies, "Does this make you want to give up?"

I understand how strange and confusing this teaching can be. It is unlike any other teaching in the world. This doesn't work the way an instructor teaches calculus to a student. The calculus teacher will impart principles and rules to begin. Spiritual teaching is going to take something away from the student, leaving him with nothing to cling to, nothing to hold onto. That's the total purpose of the teaching.

Again I say I know this sounds strange, but in order for the idea of *me* as the *doer* to go, it can't be otherwise. This teaching starves the ego down to nothing, until everything is seen to be God. I'm hopeful that after reading this book the readers will all have anorexic egos, on the verge of starvation.

The following are quotes from Jesus with interpretations as I understand them. To know Jesus, you must consume him.

Jesus' Sayings

Jesus was a fully realized spiritual teacher who walked from town to town teaching about what he called entering the Kingdom of Heaven.

Luke 17:20-21: "When the Kingdom of Heaven comes it will not come as a way to be seen. No one will say, 'Look, here it is,' or 'there it is,' because the Kingdom of Heaven is within you." Jesus was answering the Pharisees, who were educated men of that time, pointing the seeker directly back within himself. Jesus fiercely shows us that heaven is not an actual place but instead is referring to a deep, profound understanding that cannot be put into words. When he says the Kingdom of Heaven, he is pointing to the pure, choiceless, awareness that you are.

Jesus always spoke about the kingdom using parables. The reason for this is because entering the kingdom is prior to words, prior to thought, prior to manifestation. You are the kingdom itself, and when consciousness fully expands, or let's say rises, and the sense or feeling that you are a separate, individually conscience entity vanishes and you know yourself beyond the mind as pure consciousness itself, this is entering the Kingdom of Heaven. This is what Jesus meant when he asked:

Luke 13:20: "With what shall I compare the Kingdom of God? It is *like* this. A woman takes some yeast and mixes it with a bushel of flour until the whole batch of dough rises." Notice that Jesus used the words, "it is *like* this," not it is exactly this.

Jesus taught that in order to have the understanding he called entering the kingdom of God you must let go of everything and surrender your idea of free will to God.

It is interesting to note that in the Jewish culture at that time, yeast was seen as unclean. Jesus, having been raised as a Jew, surely would have known this. I believe he purposely put it in there to show that everything is God, and that this was just a law that came from ego.

Luke 16:15: "For the things that are considered great value by man are worth nothing in God's sight." Jesus used the words "God's sight," not meaning that God has eyes, but as a reference to what you are, pure choiceless awareness. By not labeling things as good or bad and letting go of attachments to material things is how awakening happens. He again makes reference to this in:

Luke 18:24: "How much harder it is for a rich person to enter the kingdom of God than for a camel to go through the eye of a needle." Attachment to things leads to suffering. Identification with those things leads to even more suffering. If we had just purchased a new house, we would say to someone, "Look, this is my new house," and on the outermost level this would be true. But on a much deeper level, this is not true at all; it belongs to God. This may seem to be a contradiction, but it is not; both statements are true. Another example is the old test for optimism or pessimism: the water glass. Some people may see the glass of water half full, while others see it as half empty. The mind always wants to see things one way or the other. Two people could argue for an hour, one saying half full, the other saying half empty. But a mind that does not see divisions sees the glass as half full and half empty at the same time. So it is both.

When an identity is created through possessions, that illusory identification is solidified even more. This is *my* car. This is *my* huge high definition television that's 79 inches and is the biggest on the block. This is *my* new leather living room set from France. Me, me, me. Mine, mine, mine. It is mankind's biggest problem for almost all of mankind's ills—poverty, homelessness, war, greed, hatred, revenge, jealousy, and on and on; they all have their roots in the worst one—fear. Fear is the seed of all calamities brought about by mankind, yet fear is not the seed itself. The seed is the idea that we are separate from God, and with this idea comes the wickedness and mother of all evil, free will.

That last sentence about free will, I'm sure, will anger at least a few people. So right now is your chance, now with that anger flowing through you, surrender and ask yourself, who is it that has become angry? The reason for this anger is that the ego, or sense of the separate entity-doer, wants to be in control. It wants to perpetuate itself. It wants to be in control and live on so badly it even makes up ideas and stories about living on after the body dies. To some, giving up the idea of control and free will feels like you're dying. That is exactly what is happening. It may be painful, but remember, you must "die" in order to be "reborn." I am not writing of a physical death, but the death of the *me* who likes to play God. When the idea of being a separate, created, individual doer dies, we are truly reborn into the kingdom, and though it may take some time, when the last piece is in place, it will be like a flash of lightning, and a joy and peace that is unparalleled will be with you in the deepest depths of your being. Although like a stormy ocean, the water may sometimes be turbulent up top, with waves and thunder and lightning, deeper down there will always be a calm stillness.

In some spiritual practices, with Jesus, and in some parts of India, some people will give everything away and beg in the streets for food, so they are not attached or identified with any belongings. Even though you give everything you own away and are totally poor and homeless and have no possessions, if you still think yourself to be a person who is super spiritual because you have given everything away and have nothing, it has done you no good at all. The identity to the body is still there, still strong, and you have not surrendered your will to God, even though all you own is the clothing on your back. Sometimes giving everything away helps the seeker; sometimes it does not.

What good is it to be homeless if you still believe yourself to be a person, still in charge with free will? It would be better to live in a huge house with many things, as long as you know they are on loan from God. True surrender comes from within.

It is the *attachment* to things, the identifying with those things, that brings the suffering. So poor or rich, homeless or living in a mansion, having many things of having nothing, is not important. What is important is surrender. With that having been said, here is a saying about Jesus, talking about letting go and giving up everything. It is taken from Al Ghazali, revival of the religious sciences, from the book *The Lost Sayings of Jesus*, translation by Andrew Phillip Smith: Jesus used to take with him nothing but a comb and a jug. One day, seeing a man comb his beard with his fingers, Jesus cast away his comb. Another day, seeing a man drink out of a river with his hands, Jesus threw away the jug. In order for the understanding to flower, attachment to everything must be given up so that the identity to form can dissolve.

Luke 19:26: "To every person who has something, even more will be given, but the person who has nothing, even the little that he has will be taken away from him." Jesus makes reference to the "glorious nothingness" by pointing to the timeless, formless, identity-less light of pure awareness that you are at your source. Jesus also comments in the gospel according to Thomas: "Split a piece of wood and I am there; lift up the stone and there you will find me." Notice that when you split a piece of wood or lift up a stone nothing is there. Jesus uses this beautiful example to point to your original origins.

The word *nothing* can seem nihilistic because the opposite of nothing is something, but the *nothing* that he speaks of has no opposite and is used only to point back to that which is prior to even oneness. Jesus taught people to not judge and to be non-violent. He taught forgiveness. He said, "Love thy neighbor as thyself," because in the utmost, deepest sense you *are* your neighbor, you *are* the one conscious presence. Jesus often spoke about compassion. These practices can help to heal the heart, slow down the mind and break down the illusory identity that has built up over time. Slowing down the mind and having compassion and forgiveness leads to a pure heart and God-realization.

Matthew 5:18: "Blessed are those who are pure in heart, for they shall see God." When Jesus spoke about being "saved," he was speaking about the darkness of egoic delusion. Being saved means you have awakened to the understanding that all is God, and now know yourself as the "light" of pure awareness. You have no shape, no form and no identity. You are truly one–one without a second. The truth shall set you free–the truth that you are not this body or this mind or this intellect or this identity. When this is realized, you (the light) are free of the divine hypnosis of separateness, transcending above the opposites of good and bad. Entering the kingdom is a bliss that knows no opposite.

All of Jesus' teachings were, in essence, practices, or training. So you practice forgiveness. You practice loving people unconditionally, which means loving them regardless of their actions toward you or other people. Loving just for the sake of loving. You practice letting go of your anger. Then after a certain amount of time—and it's different for each and every person— all your practices will become suddenly effortless, and whatever is needed for you in your life will already be there, waiting.

The process of awakening can be scary and at times make you feel uneasy. After all, there is an undoing taking place, an undoing of everything that has ever led to a false, separate identity. But after the spontaneous event of enlightenment, when your training is complete, you too can help with the awakening process in other organisms.

Luke 6:40: "No pupil is greater than his teacher, but every pupil, when he has completed his training, will be like his teacher."

John 14:12: "He who believes in me will also do the works that I do." Jesus knew things of the world will never bring lasting peace. Jesus said that after the happening of realization:

John 16:33: "The world will make you suffer. But be brave, for I have defeated the world!" Wow! What an incredible statement that is. What he is saying here is that because of his complete and total surrendering to God, the things of the world no longer have any kind of major effect on him. Although he may still feel hunger or sadness or pain, they no longer carry the same energy that they once did. He has truly been reborn, handed over to unicity, and has become the Teflon messiah because nothing sticks to him any longer.

In order to enter the Kingdom of Heaven, it should be the most important thing in your life, other than the bare necessities of living. Your mind must be as Buddhists call it "one-pointed." An example I have heard is if you were being held under water and were struggling to get a breath of air, the only thing you would be thinking about would be that one breath of air. There would be nothing coming up bothering you from your past, no worries about the future. You would be enmeshed in the now, the present moment, not thinking of anything else.

Jesus repeatedly told people to "give away" everything and follow, or listen deeply, to what he was teaching. He taught to never give up hope and to never give up searching for the kingdom within.

Luke 11:9: "Ask, and it will be given to you. Seek, and you will find. Knock, and it will be opened to you." Jesus tells us what the outcome of asking, seeking and knocking will bring:

Matthew 5:6: "Blessed are those who hunger and thirst for righteousness, for they will be satisfied."

The ego will not go quietly. Awakening to the self can be temporarily painful. Spiritual training will loosen the foundations of belief structures that have been in place for possibly decades, and when this occurs the body-mind organism can get a little agitated, to say the least.

Matthew 5:10: "Blessed are those who are persecuted for righteousness' sake, for theirs is the Kingdom of Heaven."

Pointing to the truth of your true nature, or source, can be a little bit tricky sometimes, and if done too aggressively, anger or even hatred can arise in the seeker very quickly. When you begin to let go of beliefs—beliefs that make up your identity—and when they start to crumble, who you "think" you are is dying. This is the reason for the saying in:

Matthew 5:11: "Blessed are you when men revile you and persecute you and utter all kinds of evil against you falsely."

In order to know the *self*, forgiveness, selflessness, and especially humility are essential. There follows another saying from Al Ghazali, from *The Lost Sayings of Jesus*. A disciple asked Jesus, "What action is just?" He answered, "That of whoever works for God without desiring that anyone should praise him for it."

Luke 6:27: "But I tell you who hear me—Love your enemies, do good to those who hate you, bless those who curse you, and pray for those who mistreat you." Jesus shows us, quite clearly the importance of forgiveness for the seeker. Humility also helps to loosen the illusory grip the ego has.

Luke 9:46: "A few disciples were arguing as to which one was the greatest."

Luke 9:48: Jesus answered, "He who is least among you all is the greatest."

Matthew 5:33-37: "Don't swear by heaven, or earth, or Jerusalem; do not even swear by a single hair white or black, because everything is God's will. Just say yes or no. Anything else comes from the 'evil one.'"

Many times Jesus referred to the ego as "the evil one."

Just as the Buddha said, "Have no opinions," Jesus is telling us that by postulating, swearing or having opinions on good or bad and right or wrong, we are just enflaming the sense of separateness, and once again playing God. You are the source, and the source is you. The source of all things. Jesus used the word father, and meant it as source. The father produces sperm. Sperm is a seed. The seed of a gigantic redwood tree is considered its source. So father = sperm = seed = source. This is what Jesus is pointing to in:

John 14:11: "Believe me when I say that I am in the father [source] and the father [source] is in me." Remember we are using words to point to that which can't be explained with words.

John 16:25: "I have used figures of speech to tell you these things."

In the Gospel of the Nazarenes, in Jerome, Dialogue against Pelagius 3:2, we find two very important things being said by Christ. He said, "If your brother has sinned with a word and has apologized to you, receive him seven times in a day." His disciple Simon said to him, "Seven times in a day?" The lord replied and said to him, "Yes, I tell you, even as many as seventy times seven times. For in the prophets, too, the word of sin was found, even after they were anointed with the Holy Spirit."

In the canonical Bible you will find the first part of this saying (Matthew 18:22), but you will not find the last sentence because the church wanted to portray Jesus as perfect and wanted to use a dirty four-letter word, *only*, son of God. The anointed one translates to "the Christ."

Jesus is telling us that the prophets were anointed with the Holy Spirit, which means consciousness had recognized itself. But there was not a full transcendence, for the word *sin* was used, that is, the mark was still being missed. Nevertheless, it is still true that means anyone, man or woman, can be exactly like Jesus was, with the same depth of understanding. He means what he says when he comments that every pupil can be like his teacher. The second part of the sentence "The word of sin was found" means that even after enlightenment, because we still have a body to contend with, we are not going to be super human and will still say or do the "wrong" thing sometimes. Also, as the very beginning of the statement reads, it is forgiveness that wipes the slate clean, not only for the forgiven, but for the forgiver as well.

Before going any further I would like to add something to the prior statement. The definition of the word sin is: "To miss the mark." So the one and only sin there can be is to believe the idea that you are separate from God, for if you see yourself as the doer, the thinker, the free-willer, the mark has certainly been missed. Jesus knew this and probably would have said it to his closest and more *advanced* students. But any good teacher of anything must meet the students where they are, not feeding pearls to swine. So seeing that in this statement Jesus was speaking to a crowd of people, many whom he might not have known well, he may have used the word sin in a way that meant good and bad, to reach this larger audience. This is why I put quotation marks around the word *wrong*, because there truly is no right or wrong, only the opinions of mankind.

John 10:30: "The father and I are one." Jesus was accused of blasphemy for saying this, but what he was saying was that he is not only Jesus the person, but that his true nature is the father, or source, as well. When Jesus responded to those who accused him of blasphemy, it was a spectacular saying of pure *Vedanta*, in the sense that God and the God spirit are in everything, no matter how small. But the point will be missed completely if not seen from a place of depth and understanding.

John 10:34-38: "It is written in your own law that God says you are gods. We know that what the scripture says is true forever; and God called these people gods, the people to whom his message was given. As for me, the father chose (or sanctified) me and sent me into the world. How then can you say that I blaspheme because I said that I am the son of God? We are all the sons and daughters of God whether it is revealed or not."

When enlightenment hits and everything is now seen as God, this is what he means by the saying "the people to whom his message was given." The message is the understanding that there is no you as a doer, and that everything is the source or God. The next line, "as for me, the father chose me and sent me into the world," Jesus is saying that through the body mind organism named Jesus, God has realized itself, meaning he has entered the Kingdom of Heaven. He does *not* mean that a being in the sky has made a decision to send a particular person named Jesus into the world, thus making him the father's *only* son. This is why in the next sentence Jesus asks, "How then can you say I blaspheme because I said I am the son of God?" Notice that Jesus did not say *only* son of God. He is speaking generally, saying we are all the children of the source, but to understand this you need to have this double point of view. The seekers who wanted to stone him did not understand the true depth of his saying and took it as though Jesus was saying that he, his person, was God incarnate and in relation to their persons, they were not God.

Jesus finishes up by saying, "The father is in me, and I am in the father." This is a beautiful saying of non-dualism, meaning that everything is *one*. But in their ignorance—a word the Buddha would have used—they became angry and tried to seize him, but he slipped out of their hands, probably barely making it out of there with his life. Note that the word ignorance means "not knowing." It does not mean stupid or that the people were not intelligent.

Many stories, myths and legends have been added to the Bible over the centuries to portray Jesus as superhuman and the *only* son of some man-like god in the sky. Although Jesus calls himself the Son of God, he personally never calls himself the *only* son of God. The word *only* was put in the Bible by either the authors of the gospels or by other people centuries later who rewrote the Bible. The resurrection of Christ is when his true nature was realized through the body-mind organism named Jesus.

As can be seen in the Gospel of Philip, saying #21, "They err who say the lord first died and then arose. First he arose, and then he died. If someone does not first achieve the resurrection, is he not dead already?" The author of Philip is obviously stating that when your true nature is realized, you are being resurrected. In the last sentence, Philip is stating that if you do not understand your true nature, you will be "dead" or "die" in the sense that thinking yourself to be separate from God is "death," in the spiritual sense, not the physical sense.

John 6:35: "I am the bread of life. He who comes to me will never be hungry. He who believes in me will never be thirsty." Is Jesus made of banana bread? Is Jesus, the person, a liquid and not a solid? Certainly not. Let us, together, explore the meaning of this saying.

As a true seeker of truth, we hunger for knowledge and are thirsty for answers. What Jesus is saying to his students is that if you listen carefully to what he is saying, reviewing it over and over in your mind, after the revelation of truth, you will no longer be hungry for spiritual knowledge. Your thirst will be quenched when the answer, which is the total unicity of God, if fulfilled when the understanding of your true nature is revealed through a final, spiritual revelation called entering the Kingdom of Heaven, as he put it. Jesus' saying he is the bread of life means that this revelations has already happened *through* him, not *to* him, and once it happens through you, you can rest, for your quest to know the truth will be completed. Once this spontaneously occurs, learning about things in life will still go on as they did before, for enlightenment is about spiritual knowledge, and learning about worldly things will continue the way they did before enlightenment.

17
Religious Rant

Mindless blind faith and hope are the last refuge for the shallow spiritual teacher. If anyone presenting himself as a spiritual teacher (e.g., priest, rabbi, guru, preacher, pastor) tells you just "have faith"—not because he is wise and is telling you to have patience because through your self-investigation results will come, but because he himself doesn't know the answer and doesn't truly have peace within—run like a thief in the night. A true spiritual guide, selfless in action, would teach the seeker from his *own* personal firsthand experience.

A true spiritual leader would show a seeker how to learn the *art* of acceptance instead of fearfully commanding him to "have faith." A fearless spiritual guide would then teach the first step of investigation of free will; second step, practicing acceptance; finally, culminating with contentment of "what is" in any given moment. Never would the student be asked to just have "blind faith," which leaves the seeker unfulfilled and lost. Wishing and hoping will leave you in a sad quagmire of restlessness and uncertainty. Only looking within will give you peace. Do not accept these perverted answers. Don't stop seeking or asking.

If a Guru asks you to have faith it should only be for a relatively short time for you will start to see the unraveling process happening on its own, on your own, by yourself.

Dive deep within, remembering the words of a great sage from the middle east:

Knock and the door will be opened.
Seek and you will find.
Ask and you shall receive.

18
Don't Abuse Memory

Memory is only to be used sparingly. Memory is never to be used so that suffering happens in the present moment. Try to memorize that!

When you think of things about the past it is called memory.

When you think of things about the future, it is called imagination.

When you bring Awareness to the now, "thinking" just happens, *spontaneously*.

19
Acceptance

*D*o without looking for results. In that state of acceptance, without bringing awareness to the results, you may find that what you wanted to have happen occurs more often than when you looked and wanted and desired certain results.

Remember to pull away from your thoughts; not one of them is too important.

The universe always stays exactly the same. Constantly moving.

You are not the world. You are what makes the world exist—the very awareness of it!

20
Justified Revenge

L et us forgive and love everyone and everything. There are some people who seek to do harm to others. How will you treat them? How will you feel in your heart about those people who seek to do harm to others? If you hate them and wish to seek justified revenge against them, have you not become just like them? The rewards of unconditional forgiveness are beyond limits, which is why, in my opinion, it is the most difficult task you will ever have to accomplish.

Now let me be perfectly clear about this. I do *not* think people who hurt or kill other people should be left to roam around committing the same crimes over and over again. But I refuse, with every cell of my being, to hold any anger, hatred or sense of revenge in my heart against them. What good will it do me? As soon as we start to judge people based on their actions, we are saying we know more than God.

Ironically, when I say to people that we should forgive those who have done harm against us, the people whom I tell to forgive show anger and even hatred toward me! It is as though they need my anger to sustain theirs. When I was a younger man, in my 20s, I was violent and angry. I would say and even sometimes *do* "bad" things to people and, of course, there were people who told me I was terrible and disgusting.

Now I am in my early 40s and my life has done a complete 180. Where there was hatred, now there is kindness. Where there was anger, now there is acceptance. Where there was fear, there is now contentment, and where there was judging and blaming others there is now unconditional love. But something very strange that I did not expect has come with my turned-around attitude toward life. It seems to me that when I speak about forgiveness and unconditional love, people seem to still get upset with me—sometimes even more so than when I was a miserable wretch.

Hatred and justification are a potent mixture. We all know it is "wrong" to hurt an "innocent" person. By innocent I mean the victim had done nothing to his or her attacker. For example, a poor, helpless, older woman walking into Wal-Mart is viciously beaten by a young man fiending for drugs; he steals her last 50 dollars so he can go get high. Hearing about such a heinous act would probably make anyone sick to his stomach, and so because it is such a senseless act of brutality, the justification for hatred and revenge goes through the roof. Do I believe the man who did that should be put in jail? Yes! But how would I benefit by hating him in my heart?

I know there are going to be people who read this and become angry with me. To them I say, I love you, and I understand how difficult it is to have love and forgiveness in your heart for someone who would commit such a vile act as stated in the example. But I think the confusion about forgiveness lies in the notion that it is for the perpetrator. It is not. Forgiveness is for *you!* You do not lose anything by forgiving someone in your heart; *you* gain by forgiving. The person you are forgiving doesn't even have to know you have forgiven him; hell, he doesn't even need to know you exist! Of course if someone close to you hurts you and then comes to apologize and you tell him you forgive him, it will probably make him feel better. But forgiveness and unconditional love—love with no conditions—brings you, the forgiver, a peace and contentment that, for me, is truly indescribable.

Forgiveness and unconditional love are not weakness, but strength. Think about how much violence and crime would be wiped out if we as a people could learn to love ourselves more, thus being able to forgive immediately and then banishing justified revenge from our society. Let's say someone does some kind of harm to your brother, and then you, your brother and your cousin go out to hurt that person. Let's say the original attacker has his younger, innocent brother with him when the "justified revenge" takes place. So now this "innocent" kid gets beat up or worse, just because he happened to be standing next to the original attacker. Thus that one crime has just tripled into three crimes. Can you see how it starts to spiral out of control? The only answer is love. Love for yourself, unconditional love for the attacker—a love which leads to forgiveness, which blocks "justified revenge."

21
How Is It That I Know I Exist?

Sounds flowing through the silence,
Listen! Listen, can you hear?
Outwardly turned, your mind decays.
Turn around and face your fear.

Will you run little rabbit—run, run, run?
Worried it's the bogey man who's about to come?
Have you run away your entire life?
It's time to turn around and begin to fight,
Fight, fight, with all of your might.
It is a rather amusing plight!
Fight and fight till you fight no more,
Then surrender to the open door.
Once inside, still work to do,
Only not by a me nor by a you.
Give it away, give it all away
Give up the past, give up the future

Surrender your life.

Deny that form is reality.
A knowing that's beyond conceptuality

You can handle the truth, so let's begin.

Collect your desires and turn them within,
Accept your faults and your fears,
Don't worry about those flowing tears,
Accept nothing other than full realization—
The only way, by my calculation.

This is truth.

Haunting, haunting is this life.
It need not be filled with so much strife.
Unending happiness is an illusion.
When will you come to this conclusion?
If "I am the body" is your greatest clarity,
The ego fills you with never-ending vanity.
An idea, a concept controlled by the matrix,
How many times do I have to state this?
How can you wake up from an illusory dream?
By seeing that things are not what they seem.
Know thyself in the deepest sense.
Jump down, come over! Stop sitting on the fence.
Life's just one big roller coaster ride;
Lasting happiness is found inside.

Your true nature holds up against any situation.
What are you willing to give up for it?
What are you willing to surrender to it?

What about your supposed identity?
Thinking you're a person—that's truly insanity.
"I've been born," the worst profanity.
A bunch of habits strung together by memory,
That's all your identity is anyway.
Once the alarm rings there is no snooze.
Believing you're a person you can only lose
Unlimited potential, unable to fill
The understanding; consume you it will.

You are ready for the truth.

I come not to bring peace, but with a sword
To carry you, bring you further toward
Not to the end, but to the beginning.
Hark, are those the angels I hear singing?
Lose yourself, lose yourself! Let the game begin.
The direction, it's not outward; the direction is in.
Are you ready to die, die to be reborn?

A physical death, that you may mourn,
But the death of the ego is a beautiful thing.
It is that which makes you cling.
A misty, fog-like sea of perception,
True life, the source is prior to conception,
The feeling of presence, it spontaneously shows up.
Even Jesus asked the father to take away his cup.
Although enlightenment is the greatest of the great,
As long as the body is here we are all still bait,
For the world to use anyway it sees fit,
So for the moment we must all bite the bit.
What is registering this presence
That comes and goes on its own?
The intellect can't grasp it
Although it can be known.

This is truth.
You are ready for the truth.

Potential and actual—
Two sides of the same game
Couldn't be more different
Yet completely the same.
I hurt with you
And feel your pain.
No work to do. The battle is already won.
Just see clearly as if it were the sun.
I am the father, son and the holy spirit.
Don't step away, run, no need to fear it.
As are you, the trinity is one,
The father, the holy ghost and the son.
The journey awaits yet it has begun,
Do not stop till you're completely done.
The world is full of angry sleep walkers,
The kings of gossip, the top of the talkers,
But be careful when you up them wake;
Have compassion for they are fake.
It could be dangerous interrupting their business

If you preach love, kindness and forgiveness.
Put a bulls eye on your back;
Sit and wait for them to attack.
It may be better to wait with your horse sense
As they come to you bringing their pretense.
Very great your patience must be.
Until you wait for them to see
For such delusion there is no need
So wait in the silence and plant a seed
Knowing full well there is no doer.
I threw my identity into the sewer
A random occurrence, a random event,
A random thought, into the silence I went,
Never to return. I'm on the far shore.
Surrender now to that open door.
Die, die, you wicked adversary,
Pay the man to ride across on the ferry,
Cross the ocean of existence
Never turn back, complete persistence,
Fear will come and fear will go,
The only thing that ruins the show.

You are ready for truth.

Face your fear, it's not that bad,
For if you don't your life will be sad
You have no attributes, this is truth.
Just keep searching, you'll find the proof.
The veil has been lifted, now I can see,
There is no such thing as a *you* or a *me*.
It's all and only God, in the deepest sense.
Are you once again, sitting on the fence?
Do these writings strike a chord?
Can you feel it or are you bored?
As for life you must learn to bend,
For in the beginning you will find the end.
Bitter it is so just spit it out,
Let go of your identity, your name, your clout.

Be not afraid, a guide will come,
As life beats away to the sound of a drum.
Deny reality to the idea of a *me*
How much better life will be.
Be free of the shackles, the ones that bind.
Free yourself now and open your mind.
Don't be fooled by a form and a shape.
Look within, the greatest escape.
Dive right in, the water's fine.
So go beyond, don't toe the line.
Purge, purge, burn it all away,
Just enjoy life and learn to play.
Like a sickness, a disease of the mind,
Where is the *me*? Can you find?
Take a look; it won't be there.
Oh, how powerful is the Guru's stare.
What does it matter who's there to care?
Your true nature? It hides in the air.

Illusion deceives, it doesn't seem to care.
You can handle the truth.

Emptiness, emptiness calling me home.
For all those years all I did was roam.
Dancing forms no longer confine
Emptiness, my sweet valentine.
Effortless detachment, yet forms still dance,
The world's still spinning, but now seen with a glance.
Erased! It's gone. Nothing is there.
Eternally, witnessing, without a care.
Potential now, potential then,
No longer in God's lion's den.
Light pervading knows no dark,
Manifestation, just a little spark.
Sweet, sweet sea of perception,
Yes, you are prior to conception.
Imagining bonds, Imagining dreams,
No, you are not what you seem.

You know no boundaries, this is truth.
Investigate, investigate, there will be proof.
Ask yourself, *I am who*?
Do not let matter rule over you.
Space it seems—it seems to affect
Randomly, randomly, the variables connect.
There is no path, there is no road.
Pure awareness, it is my abode.
Wake up! Wake up! Sit up and look!
Nothing needs to be done, just don't bite the hook.
If you want it, just empty your cup.
Your mind will open; it all clears up.
Watch, look and listen to your heart.
Follow it relentlessly until the clouds part.
Give your life to this endeavor,
Don't be fooled and think you're clever.
Memory can trap you and the future, too.
So always remember, there is no *you*!

22
Separateness

The sense of separateness—what is it? Who is sensing the separateness? When this sense of separateness falls away like a discarded robe, what is left is what has always been and what will always be:

> Wholeness
> Completeness
> Fullness
> Lacking not
> Ever-present, pure awareness
> Uncaused
> Unsupported
> Pure Being

Being aware, in the present moment, of your surroundings—e.g., your breath—can temporarily take you out of the thought flow. In the Absolute Space beyond the mind there is stillness. When this is "realized," peace and love in your heart are mainstays, as well as fearlessness.

Why search for love when you are love? Why look to outside sources to make you complete when it is impossible? You are already complete. So Just Be Your Self, not knowing anything or becoming anything.

Now I'm not saying that people should start divorcing each other, only that true love has no opposite. The source is beyond male and female. It is the beginning and the end, and you are that very Source. Love that defines you is not true love.

Egoic love has an opposite. From an Egoic perception, Love and Hate are separate. Although they appear to be at opposite ends of the spectrum, they are really just the outermost limits of connectiveness, and so *they* appear to be *two*, but they are really one. For one cannot exist without the other.

23
Here Are Some Other
Things I Have Learned
(#2)

• Peace is better than war, but unfortunately sometimes war is what can bring the peace.

  Question: What kind of country would America be if our national anthem were "Imagine," by John Lennon, instead of a song about war, no matter how inspiring or patriotic it might be?

• People who are selfless and have completely surrendered to God can never be affected for more than a few minutes by people who act selfishly or show anger toward them.

• I can talk about my feelings, show love and forgiveness and even cry sometimes and be even more of a man.

• It is better to give than to receive.

• A tooth for a tooth leaves the world without a smile.

• As important as it is not to judge others, it is more important not to judge yourself.

• Communication, respect and love are the very foundation of any relationship.

• Once the foundation has been set, forgiveness is what keeps any relationship going strong.

• Once you fully surrender to God, nothing is that big a deal

- The best way to teach somebody something is by example.

- In addition to sharing the same planet, we also all share the same consciousness.

24
Consciousness

I am not the Tree, but what makes it grow.
I am not the Fish, but what makes it swim.
I am not the Wind, but what pushes it.
I am not the Air, but what makes it breathable.
I am not the Land, but that which holds it together.
I am not the Animals, but what makes them run.
I am not the Humans, but what makes them think.
I am the Conscious Presence; I am everywhere.
I am the Consciousness without [the Presence]; I am nowhere.

You ARE prior to knowing you are, and you still *are* even when you don't know you are anymore. That should clear things up for you. For whom?

See it all as one. You don't arise separately from the universe; everything arises at once. Although there is separateness between physical things, it is all made out of the same building material, consciousness.

Everything is consciousness. The tree is not in consciousness. The tree IS consciousness.

Ya know how sometimes on the inside of a white tee shirt it reads 100% cotton? Well, if you could look at the label on everything that was manifest, down to the tiniest atom, although they would be very small tags, they would read 100% consciousness.

25
The (Coptic) Gospel of Thomas
Interpretation of Translated Sayings

For this part of the book I have written and interpreted the Coptic Gospel of Thomas. Let us begin with a brief background and how it came to be known. The first discovery of the Gospel of Thomas occurred in the late 1800s on Oxyrhynchus papyrus, written in Greek. Some of it was in fragments. But then near the town of Nag Hammadi, Egypt, in 1945, some people digging for fertilizer uncovered a sealed jar containing ancient writings including a complete version of the Gospel of Thomas, written in Coptic (ancient Egyptian). I will be using the English translation of the Coptic version of the Gospel of Thomas. Thus I will be interpreting the meaning of the sayings, not translating them from one language to another.

In this gospel there are 114 sayings Jesus said to Thomas, who some scholars believe was Jesus' twin brother. Whether this means Thomas was his physical twin or spiritual twin is unknown. What I personally like about it is that there is nothing about any resurrection, immaculate conception or crucifixion—only deep, profound, sayings that are of such beauty and depth that they can leave the reader breathless.

The Emperor Constantine, who put together the Bible at the Council of Nicea in 325 A.D. must have left this brilliant piece of material out of the canonical Bible because he wanted a Bible that just told a story about Jesus for people to follow. Thomas's gospel, if understood correctly, can wake the reader/seeker from his slumber, showing him he has no need for a church. That was the last thing the child-murdering Constantine would have wanted, for through the body-mind-organism named Constantine, the "evil one" as Jesus put it, was quite apparent. The gospel begins by saying these are the secret sayings the living Jesus spoke and which Didymas Judas Thomas wrote down.

Saying #1

And he said, "Whoever finds the interpretation of these sayings will not experience death."

What this saying does not mean is that the body will not die and "you" will live on as a person or some individual soul. Everything that has a beginning has an end, and when the body dies, that's it. But your true nature is not this body, nor is it this mind. Thus, when we have the realization that you are the beginningless source, and since the source has no beginning, it cannot have an end or "experience death."

Saying #5

Jesus said, "Recognize what is in your sight, and that which is hidden from you will become plain to you. For there is nothing hidden which will not become manifest."

It is my understanding that what Jesus is saying to his students here is that to know yourself, you must first know what you are not. Recognize that you are not the body or the mind. Recognize that you are not the thought flow or the memory. Recognize that you are not the identity or the body. Then what is hidden from you will become plain to you. *You* will realize you are formless. *You* will know thoughts, words, or memory can never identify you, for your true nature goes beyond the spoken word. A revelation shall occur, and it will be known that you are prior to time and space, and not confined to this bag of bones you call a body. So when you recognize what you're *not* (in your sight), then your true nature (that which is hidden from you), will become known (become manifest).

Saying #14

Jesus said to them, "If you fast, you will give rise to sin for yourself; and if you pray, you will be condemned, and if you give alms, you will do harm to your spirits. When you go into any land and walk about in the districts, if they receive you, eat what they will set before you and heal the sick among them. For what goes into your mouth will not defile you, but that which issues from your mouth, it is that which will defile you."

I will break this saying down into three parts. The first part starts with the words, "If you fast," and ends with, "your spirits." To sin means to "miss the mark," the mark being it is all God. So if you fast, you may be deepening or strengthening the idea that there is a *you* there, doing some action that will make you greater or more spiritual than other people. If you pray, asking God for some type of favor, this will further add to the idea that God is separate from you, thus strengthening the "idea" of your being the doer or free-willer. If you give alms, this may make you feel more important or special, thus further trapping you in illusion.

The second part starts with the words, "when you," and ends with the words, "among them." In ancient Jewish culture there were many foods forbidden to be eaten, believed to be unclean. Jesus ignores this rule and tells his disciples to be polite and eat whatever is given to them, for some people were very poor and it would be insulting to them if you refused to eat their food because of a silly manmade belief.

Healing the sick means to spread the word of the kingdom, thus bringing people out of the darkness of egoic delusion and into the light of the glorious source, which is pure awareness.

Part three continues with a saying about the new rules about food that Jesus believed, which was that you are not unclean because you ate some delicious pulled pork but were unclean if you gossiped, judged or spoke badly about anyone. This, to this day, is still true, and I believe as long as humans walk this earth it shall be that way, regardless of any belief structures that are still in place today or in the future.

Remember, it is not what goes into you that makes you "unclean," but the words and feelings along with those words that come out of you that will "defile" you, as Jesus put it.

Saying # 17

Jesus said, I shall give you what no eye has seen and what no ear has heard and what no hand has touched and what has never occurred to the human mind."

Wow! What an awesome saying this one is. The father, or source, once again is prior to anything and everything, so it cannot be seen, it cannot be put into words, you obviously cannot touch it in anyway, and because of this it cannot be understood with the mind. But he says "I shall give you," which means that even though all those things are true, including that it cannot be understood with or occur to the mind, it can still be *known* in a miraculous, nonconceptual way through revelation. And when I say "revelation," this is not to be confused with the "Book of Revelation."

Saying #13

Jesus said to his disciples, "Compare me to someone and tell me who I am like."

Simon Peter said to him, "You are like a righteous angel."

Matthew said to him, "You are like a wise philosopher."

Thomas said to him, "Master, my mouth is wholly incapable of saying who you are like."

Jesus said, "I am not your master. Because you have drunk, you have become intoxicated

**from the bubbling spring which I have measured
out."**

In the first sentence, in which Jesus is speaking, he is testing his friends and students, to see how deep their understanding has become. In the second part of this saying, in which the three men answer Jesus, Simon Peter and Matthew show their ignorance, by seeing Jesus as a person with a separate identity, comparing him to other beings—Peter to an angel, and Matthew to a philosopher. Then Thomas, whose understanding is deeper than that of the other two men, states that he cannot compare Jesus to anyone or even anything.

Jesus compliments Thomas by telling him, "I am not your master." That's because a deep understanding has arisen in Thomas because of the teaching Jesus has "measured out," that Thomas's understanding has now reached the point of Jesus' understanding, so to speak, and the depth of their understanding is now equal.

Saying #18
**The disciples said to Jesus, "Tell us how our
end will be."**

**Jesus said, "Have you discovered, then, the
beginning, that you look for the end? For where
the beginning is, there will the end be. Blessed is
he who will take his place in the beginning. He
will know the end and not experience death."**

When we see ourselves as a person with a body who has been born, it is only natural, at that point we should wonder how our "end" will be. But Jesus reminds them that they will have no end, because their true nature, potential, has neither a beginning nor an end. Or you could say that because your true nature is the "potential to be," that your beginning and end are wrapped up in this potential. And also that because potential is prior to births of any kind, including the birth of the universe, that you could, from that point of view, so to speak, never experience death.

Saying #31

Jesus said, "No prophet is accepted in his own village. No physician heals those who know him."

Usually a doctor will not treat his own family, for he has an emotional attachment to them, and that attachment will affect the way he sees or views the patient and will not be able to be detached while treating his patient. Thus the risk of making a mistake is much higher.

The lesson about the prophet is somewhat the reverse. The townspeople have known the prophet's background and his early life. They have seen him grow up, and because they see themselves as persons, they will see the prophet as a person, knowing intimate details of his life. Because of this, it will be much harder for the prophet to teach those people about the untruth of their identity and the truth about their formlessness.

The people had known Jesus before he realized his true nature and knew him when he himself was stuck in illusion. The effect of the teaching on these people would have been greatly diminished, for if they had seen Jesus running home to his mommy crying at five years of age, how now would they understand his teaching that he is really timeless, formless and choiceless, pure awareness, and not that little boy they knew when he was growing up?

Saying #49

Jesus said, "Blessed are the solitary and elect, for you will find the kingdom. For you are from it, and to it you will return.

In the canonical Bible you read many times about going to or entering the kingdom, but never do you hear that you are from it! Once again I say Constantine knew this gospel was much deeper and more profound than the other gospels, and if he is telling a story about heaven being a physical place you go to when you die, he would have had a hard time explaining how you came from it! If you are solitary and as a seeker of truth have fasted from the world, stopped believing that you are a person that's been born, denied that your memory defines you, refuse to see yourself as separate from God and totally and completely with every cell of your being, surrendered to God, you are truly blessed. When your true nature is realized, the realization that you are the kingdom itself, then you know yourself to be the source of all things, including your body; you will know that as well as coming from the source, all things return to the source.

Saying #56

Jesus said, "Whoever has come to understand the world has found only a corpse, but whoever has found a corpse is superior to the world.

Once again, understanding the world means the knowing of your true nature has been understood. With this understanding you know you are not this body; henceforth you have found a corpse, or another word that could be used is robot. In other words you are "dead" to the pull of the world that was once there, when you thought yourself to be separate from it.

And so with this new understanding that you are not the body, you are in a sense superior to the world, for now you know your true nature is the very source of the world. He does not mean that after this understanding that the person itself is in some way superior, in comparison to other people or to physical things of the world. Also the world, the people in it, and the thoughts, feelings and emotions of your body/person are now seen in a completely different way, although nothing in the world has changed; even the concept of entering the Kingdom of Heaven—everything changes, yet everything stays the same.

Saying #61 (partial saying)

Jesus said, "I am he who exists from the undivided. Therefore I say, if he is destroyed, he

will be filled with light, but if he is divided, he will be filled with darkness."

Here in this statement, Jesus uses the word undivided to mean the source or father, as he switches back and forth, using different words to point to the absolute. The next part is so very beautiful. Destroyed means the ego, or sense of being the doer. When destroyed, it leaves a person filled with light, for now the knowledge that they are truly the light of awareness is there. But if he is divided, meaning, believes he is separate from God or divided from God, then of course he will be filled with darkness, because the belief that you are separate from God is hell, which is the ultimate darkness.

Saying #58
Jesus said, "Blessed is the man who has suffered and found life."

From most people's point of view, suffering is a bad thing, so to speak. But here Jesus tells us that a man is blessed who has suffered. This is because suffering is a major component of surrender. The more intense the suffering, the greater the surrender can be. It is the surrendering of a person's will, his life and, for true enlightenment, his very identity. When this is done there is an enormous release of that suffering. If the surrender is great enough, the entire identity of being a separate person goes; then one is filled with light and now *knows* God or the father or the source, which is the potential of all life manifested, and is life itself.

Saying #60
They saw a Samaritan carrying a lamb on his way to Judea. He said to his disciples, "This man is round about the lamb."

They said to him, "So that he may kill it and eat it."

He said to them, "While it is alive, he will not eat it, but only when he has killed it and it has become a corpse."

They said to him, "He cannot do so otherwise."

He said to them, "You, too, look for a place for yourselves within repose, lest you become a corpse and be eaten."

Whoa! That's a mouthful, and I'm not talking about the lamb. A person in hiding might say, "Call me mint jelly, 'cause I'm on the lam!"

All right, enough of that. Let us together start the exploration of this saying with one of the definitions of repose. According to Webster's New World dictionary, "To place power in the control of some person or group." What I believe Jesus is telling his students here is do not believe that you have the power or control over things. Look for a person, or in this case, God, with whom to place the power. Because if you do not realize it is all God, and you think you have free will and control, you will be dead spiritually, and if you are a corpse spiritually, you will be eaten by the world, which means you will suffer, be lost in confusion and darkness, and live a life of dichotomy instead of unicity.

Saying #95

Jesus said, "Seek and you will find. Yet, what you asked me about in former times and which I did not tell you then, now I do desire to tell you, but you do not inquire after it."

Jesus is trying to inspire and motivate his students by telling them to seek for the source in them and inquire or ask him about it. But probably because of the "level" of their understanding, in former times, possibly a few years back, Jesus did not expose the full depth of his understanding to them, for he believed it would have gone over their heads. And they were not ripe enough for it to be heard.

With this saying it appears that he wants to give them a deeper explanation of the teaching, yet it seems he believes they are still not ready for it because they are not asking him deeper questions or looking for deeper answers. This statement shows that even after enlightenment, life—especially for a Guru—can still be somewhat frustrating. It also shows us that the enlightened sage can still have a very human part to him, although I believe his frustrations wouldn't have lasted very long at all.

Saying #53

His disciples said to him, "Is circumcision beneficial or not?

He said to them, "If it were beneficial, their father would beget them already circumcised from their mother. Rather, the true circumcision spirit has become completely profitable.

As we all know, circumcision is the cutting away of the foreskin. Jesus uses this term to mean the "cutting away" of our attachments to this world, our attachments to our possessions and of course our attachments to the body, or identity, too. He was not concerned with rituals or traditions that keep the seeker further locked into identity with the body. He ate with people with whom the more "elite" people would have not associated. He preached his message to criminals, or as they put it back then, "undesirables." And even though he was a Jew, he didn't clean himself in a ritual way, which brings us to our next saying.

Saying #89

Jesus said, "Why do you wash the outside of the cup? Do you not realize that he who made the inside is the same one who made the outside?

What he is saying here, I believe, is that you are going through all this ritual bullshit, cleaning this, doing that, thinking that somehow it is going to bring you closer to God or that because of all this ritual, traditional nonsense that God is going to favor you over someone else. God is not a person! God does not pick favorites or treat people better or worse because of something you did or did not do. It is what is on the inside of you that counts. It is what comes out of you that makes you clean or unclean. You can wash the dishes as many times as you want, but if you're talking bad about someone while doing it, you are keeping the idea of being the doer, instead of surrendering that idea. Also, because God is not a person with human attributes, doing "good" things or "nice" things does not put you in any better standing with God. What unselfish or kind and loving acts will do for you is that you will not be feeding the ego anything, thus loosening the grip of the illusory idea that there is a *you* there in the first place. When this idea is finally gone, it shall be known that everything is literally God. That there is nothing but God. That there never has or ever will be anything separate from God. It is this understanding that brings peace through the organism, not to a *you*, because there is no *you*. Most people seek enlightenment because they think it will do something or bring some kind of peace to them. Enlightenment is nothing more or less than God-realizing that it is all God, for the final understanding is the dissolving of the seeker.

Saying #69

Jesus said, "Blessed are they who have been persecuted within themselves. It is they who have truly come to know the father. Blessed are the hungry, for the belly of him who desires shall be filled.

It is a true blessing to suffer deeply, for it is with most humans that until suffering has become too great to bear that there shall be no true surrender. Yet with this surrender, the surrender to the idea of yourself to God, this is where you shall find peace and grace, and it is through that peace and grace that the understanding that it is all God will arise, or as Jesus put it, know the father.

The last sentence, in my understanding, is this: That only through a deep hunger or desire for the knowledge will that knowledge appear through a revelation. Also, it is the lack of desires for things of the world that will bring peace, because when a worldly desire is fulfilled, it only creates more desire. Yet when you desire nothing, you are free, because it is desirelessness that paves the way to the absolute.

An interesting note I would like to add to the saying is in the Greek version of the Gospel of Thomas there is a somewhat different ending to saying #69. Instead of "... for the belly of him who desires will be filled," which is the Coptic (ancient Egyptian) version, the translation from the Greek reads, "... *that the stomach of someone else in want may be filled.*"

This may mean that because you have "come to know the father" you can now help to guide other people to this revelation. I use the word guide because even though I'm writing a book about it, this teaching cannot be taught in the same way another teacher teaches something. Although there are many awakenings or unravelings with which the Guru can help the student along the way, the final understanding cannot be taught or given to the student. The ultimate understanding can only happen on its own through a revelation that happens through the student. If there is anything you understand from this book, I hope it is those last two or three sentences.

There are many people out there who would love to take your money and tell your ego what it wants to hear, so be careful and be honest and sincere to yourself about yourself. Use your heart and follow it, and a competent guide will find his or her way into your life. One of my all-time favorite gurus is a man whose spiritual name is Nisargadatta Maharaj. He died in 1981, so he doesn't want anything from you, but beware—L.O.L.—he will knock the *me* right out of *you* very quickly. I recommend anything by him. I must add quickly that when I say "by him" I mean it was his students who recorded question-and-answer dialogues between 1970 and 1981 and then transferred them to books. He never wrote anything himself, and when you read those books, you start to feel as though you're sitting in that little room of his, where seekers from around the world would come to listen to him speak. His style cuts through deeply and quickly.

Saying #42
Jesus said, "Become passers-by."

What this very short saying means is that the world has a beginning, therefore it shall have an end. It is only that which has no beginning that will have no end. So do not make the world your home, so to speak, and just pass over or pass by it, for the world is transient; but your true nature is not. There is a passage, written on the wall of a mosque of all places, in India, which reads, "Jesus said, 'This world is a bridge, Pass over it, but do not build your dwelling there.'" On a wall in a mosque! Isn't that crazy? Far out, man!

Saying #27
Jesus said, "If you do not fast as regards the world you will not find the kingdom. If you do not observe the Sabbath as a Sabbath, you will not see the father."

The usual meaning of the words "to fast" means not to take in any food. Jesus uses this clever switch of the word to mean if we take in the world, see it as real and then separate from ourselves, it will create the very sense of *me* in it, and as long as the belief that there is a separate *me* in the world we, most likely, will not find the kingdom, which is the very source of manifestation itself, including the universe, the world and any idea of one in it!

As for the second sentence, it is my belief that this was added to this gospel long after Jesus walked the earth, because the fully realized person knows there is no day that is more important than any other day; there are no concrete rules to enter the kingdom, and Jesus himself broke some of the rules of the Sabbath and was accused of this several times in the Bible. On the other hand, in a universe with infinite possibilities, it is of course possible that he said this and there is some meaning to it that I am missing. I do not believe this is probable, but I can't dismiss it out of hand.

Saying #94.
Jesus said, "He who seeks will find, and he who knocks will be let in."

As I have said before, there are no concrete rules, and no one knows when the final understanding will come. But it does appear that your desire and tenacity to know yourself will help to remove some of the obstacles in the way of the realization that has always been there waiting. So keep seeking and keep knocking.

A strange twist to this teaching is that everything must be given up—every path, every discipline—which means that at some point even the seeking and knocking have to be given up. This is the paradoxical nature of the teaching, for enlightenment to happen even the quest for enlightenment has to given up at some point.

Saying #113
His disciples said to him, "When will the kingdom come?"

Jesus said, "It will not come by waiting for it. It will not be a matter of saying, 'Here is it,' or 'There it is.' Rather, the kingdom of the father is spread out upon the earth, and men do not see it."

This saying is reminiscent of the version of it in Luke 17:21-22. Yet in Luke it ends with, "*Because the Kingdom of Heaven is within you.*" This ending is saying the same thing, just in a different way. The kingdom, or the source, or the father, or whatever words you would like to use to point at it. What Jesus is saying is that finding the kingdom is not done in a linear way—in which you look for something in a forward momentum and at the end, find it. Rather the kingdom is everywhere and is the source of everything. It is not something to be found, but something to be realized, for it is already everywhere; it is just a matter of being able to see it. But as Jesus says in Luke, "It will not come in a way as to be seen." He is not talking about seeing with your eyes. He's talking about a deep, profound, intuitive revelation, and when everything finally snaps into place it shall be known in a way that the mind could never dream of or invent. Then it shall be known.

Saying #82
Jesus said, "He who is near me is near the fire, and he who is far from me is far from the kingdom."

I believe what Jesus is pointing to here is this: "He who is near me" means that whoever has listened to his teaching and has taken it in and digested it, in that person the unraveling process has begun. With this unraveling process, the idea of there being a separate *me* will eventually be burnt up or burnt out of the person, replaced with the understanding that it is all God.

In the person in whom the teaching has not stuck, been digested or has had no effect, that person will be far from Jesus, or far from his teaching, thus being far from the kingdom, which is the revelation of everything being God.

Saying #108
Jesus said, "He who will drink from my mouth will become like me. I myself shall become he,

and the things that are hidden will be revealed to him."

Boy, Jesus surely was masterful with the way he used phrases and words to speak about that which is unspeakable. They just seemed to flow right out of him, as skillfully as from a Shakespeare or a Thoreau. Let us begin with two things he said in the first sentence. If you are open to and ingest his words and teaching, letting them really sink in and hold, you are drinking from his mouth. What an awesome way to put it!

Second, and equally important, is something *any* Christian church is sure to stay far away from and avoid. Four beautiful words that could turn Christianity as we know it today on its head, breaking the grip the church has on people: "... will become like me." There it is. How beautiful and honest that statement is with such humility. At our source we are all one. The outer form itself may be different, but at our core, we are all the same. Jesus is saying we all can become like him—kind, loving, honest, with the same depth of understanding that emerged through Jesus.

It is that damned, stinkin' ego that gets in the way of our seeing the unicity of all things, of our seeing that it is all God, and that this body is nothing more than a little receiver of information, programmed spontaneously and randomly, by a very big universe and, of course, our genes and DNA.

In the second sentence he is saying once again we are all one, stating, "I, myself, shall become he," and then the "hidden" understanding of unicity will reveal itself.

Saying #51

His disciples said to him, "When will the repose of the dead come about, and when will the new world come?"

He said to them, "What you look forward to has already come, but you do not recognize it."

How can heaven be a physical place you go to when you die physically, when Jesus is telling people who are alive that it has already come? Obviously it cannot. So once again we can see why so many deep, profound writings, all circulating at the same time, would have been left out of the very small New Testament. Think about it. There are organizations selling the people a story of a good-bad dichotomy, telling you that if you're "good" you get to go to some place and live out eternity, having all of your wishes granted. They're telling you these stories to keep you in line, telling you to obey the government, making sure you don't make trouble. Now what happens if you hear about sayings like these—even entire gospels?

Obviously the people in power wanted such writings to be suppressed. They didn't fit into the story. These writings would create havoc as far as "public safety" from the POV of those in power were concerned, because the power of the authorities would be lost if people found out Jesus was really saying God could be found within. People who discovered these sayings of Jesus would know there was no need for the power structure of the church; the rules of the church didn't have to be followed, and people could keep their money, not handing it over to those in authority who were lying about Jesus' true message

It is only by the enlightened thinking of some very brave people that these sayings and gospels were saved. Thinking these writings were important enough to risk their lives to save, they hid or buried them so that we have them today. The kingdom is the source. The source has, is and always will be the potential of everything it is. It's just a matter of recognizing it. Jesus explains this to his disciples in saying #51, saying they have not recognized it. He is telling his students the kingdom has come, but that it must be seen by a way that does not include their eyes. It can be known through an intuitive revelation.

Saying #77

Jesus said, "It is I who am the light which is above them all. It is I who am the all. From me did the all come forth, and unto me did the all extend. Split a piece of wood and I am there. Lift up the stone, and you will find me there."

Before reading my interpretation it might be helpful to refer back to Chapter 7, titled "The Switch."

Okay, stay with me, here, and I will try to make this as painless as possible. In this saying, Jesus is switching around the usage of some words. In the first sentence he uses the words "I" and "light" to mean the source. Still in the first sentence he uses the words "them *all*" to mean the totality of manifestation of the entire universe. In the second sentence he uses the words "I" and "all" to mean the same thing, the source, speaking from the POV of the source.

In the third sentence he uses the word "me" now to mean the source and then twice uses the word "all" to mean the totality of manifestation, switching back the meaning. So in the third sentence speaking from the POV of the source he's saying everything comes from me, the source, and everything comes back into me, the source.

In the fourth and fifth sentences he is trying to convey to his students that the source cannot be seen with the eye, yet is everywhere, by saying if you split a piece of wood or lift up a stone you will find me there. When he says "I" and "me" in sentences four and five he is once again speaking from the point of view the source. This switching back and forth from the POV of the source to the POV of the person is common in the Hindu tradition of the teaching of enlightenment. It can add confusion to an already extremely confusing teaching, but that is just how it plays out through some teachers. Lord Krishna does this in the Gita, almost always speaking from the source.

An interesting note is that we do not find this often, if at all, in the teaching of the Buddha. What is also intriguing is that the Buddha was raised Hindu. Before the Buddha came along, there was no Buddhism or Buddhists. Maybe being raised Hindu, the Buddha saw this switching back and forth and decided to leave it out of his teachings, thinking it would further confuse the seeker, or maybe he never even thought about it, and that's just how the variables played out.

One last thing I should like to say is that it is apparent to me that Jesus uses this switch often, and it is this one thing that has made Jesus' teaching more difficult for the Western mind to pick up. I also believe that if Jesus did in fact go to India in his lost years, ages 12-29, that he studied Hinduism, not Buddhism.

Saying #15

Jesus said, "When you see one who was not born of woman, prostrate yourselves on your faces and worship him. That one is your father."
There are a few really neat things about this saying. Obviously we are all born of a woman physically, so Jesus means that when you are reborn spiritually you know your body came from another body, but your true nature is the source itself. He then tells his disciples to bow down and worship that person, which means listen to his teachings. He doesn't mean to actually worship that person, for then you would be missing the point completely.

Jesus says to a man who calls him a *good teacher*, "Why do you call me good? God alone is good." So as we can see, Jesus himself did not want to be worshiped, for worshipping a Guru will only keep the seeker further locked into identity. Jesus then goes on to say, "That one is your father," meaning that through that person the source, or as Jesus put it, the father, has been understood. It is also interesting to note that Jesus is telling and showing us that this understanding can happen through anyone. It is not just him that the understanding has come through, but it is available to anyone, thus shattering the idea that Jesus is the *only* son of the father, the source, or God, whatever name you would like to use as a pointer.

Saying #41
Jesus said, "Whoever has something in his hand will receive more, and whoever has nothing will be deprived of the little he has."
If you look at this saying from a worldly, separate person's point of view, it doesn't seem very good, or fair. From an egoic point of view, it may seem to some that Jesus is saying the rich get richer and the poor get poorer. This is not what Jesus was saying, for in the body-mind organism Jesus, the idea of there being a separate *me* had vanished and been replaced with the eyes of unicity. So, from a deep spiritual point of view the people who have something in their hands will receive more things of the world, adding to the illusory sense of being the doer. But if you continuously surrender to God the idea of being in charge, the little bit of ego left will be consumed by the fires of surrender, and there will be nothing left but God. This has always been the case, but the difference now is that it is known.

Saying #32
Jesus said, "A city being built on a high mountain and fortified cannot fall, nor can it be hidden."
I believe what Jesus is referring to here is this: Your true nature, once realized, can never be forgotten or hidden from being known ever again. Once you wake up from the dream, you can't go back, so to speak. So as life progresses, that understanding will hold up against anything thrown at you. It is intimately yours and cannot fall, once this revelation is fortified.
Another strange twist to this revelation, is that once the full surrender has occurred and the knowing that it is all God has been revealed, because of the profundity,

depth or rareness of this understanding, there can at times be a fleeting feeling of loneliness. Yet this, too, is just the play of God. It reminds me of another quote of Jesus, "Oh, Jerusalem, how I weep for you, how I wish I could put my arms around you."

Saying #97
Jesus said, "The Kingdom of the father is like a certain woman who was carrying a jar full of meal. While she was walking on the road, still some distance from home, the handle of the jar broke and the meal emptied out behind her on the road. She did not realize it; she had noticed no accident. When she reached her house, she set the jar down and found it empty."

This is another beautiful parable by Jesus pointing to the absolute reality. Let's break it down sentence by sentence. The woman carrying a jar full of meal represents the person who is living the usual life of separateness from God, thinking she is a person with, of course, free will, making decisions, having some shame and guilt, that she was born and will die.

While walking on the road or while starting her spiritual path or journey, still some distance from home—or still far away from knowing of the emptiness of potential, the handle of the jar breaks and meal begins to empty out behind her. This means her journey is now in full swing, emptying out all the things that have kept her in illusion of being the doer, although she may not even know it is happening, for she has noticed no accident.

But when she reaches home or finally realizes her true nature, she finds the jar empty. She has become empty of her identity, knowing that it is all God. That one is awesome, isn't it?

Saying #39
Jesus said, "The Pharisees and the scribes have taken the keys of knowledge (gnosis) and

hidden them. They themselves have not entered, nor have they allowed to enter those who wish to. You, however, be as wise as serpents and as innocent as doves."

What Jesus is telling his disciples is to beware of the Pharisees and scribes because of what they teach. Their twisted and perverted teaching of the dichotomy of God, of God being an enlarged person in the sky, has not allowed them to understand their true nature. They are thirsty for power and money, but not for "gnosis," which means wisdom. They have taken the keys to understanding this wisdom and hidden them through their own ignorance. Because so many people look to them for answers, those people have not found the essence of wisdom. Their teachers cannot teach them because they themselves have no true depth of understanding. Jesus tells his students to be wise and see through these teachers' ignorance but be innocent as to not upset them or argue with them or take their power away, for we all know what happened to Jesus.

That was, of course, back then when Pharisees had great power and could get you in serious trouble. Now, of course, you can speak your mind and—in most places and cases—not be put to death. Jesus is telling them they can find the keys to the kingdom inside themselves. Thus having no need for a church, if they would just seek within themselves. But alas, many of them did not and would rather have someone tell them what to believe in, rather than going through the pain of spiritual maturity, ending in a true revelation of the spirit. It seems as if not much has changed in the past 2000 years, Even the "being put to death" part.

Saying #114

Simon Peter said to them, "Let Mary leave us, for women are not worthy of life."

Jesus said, "I myself shall lead her in order to make her male, so that she too may become

a living spirit resembling you males. For every woman who will make herself male will enter the Kingdom of Heaven."

I shall leave this final saying uninterpreted for the reader to think about and interpret. Remember that no one knows when the final understanding will appear, and no one can teach it. I hope these sayings have helped unravel some concepts to allow realization of revelation to occur spontaneously. My brothers and sisters, have fun, love one another and forgive each other.

Okay, I'm just going to say one thing about #114. Enlightenment can happen to anyone, male or female.

III

The Kingdom of Heaven

26
The Story of
Adam and Eve

He told him, "You may eat the fruit of any tree in the
garden, except the tree that gives knowledge of what is
Good and what is Bad.

—*Genesis 2:16-17*

The story of Adam and Eve is a warning against labeling anything as good or bad. In the absence of labeling anything as good or bad, there is Paradise.

What is Paradise? Well, I'm glad you asked that question. Paradise is the outcome of acceptance of what *is* in the moment. Do not disagree, as if it shouldn't be happening, whatever "it" may be. If you investigate how quickly your mind automatically labels things, events, situations, people, you may find you disagree more than you know. That's okay, because the recognition of it is definitely a movement out of it. Be passionately dispassionate and witness the mind hitting the "accept" or "reject" buttons. Replace those two outcomes with "this is spontaneously happening"! Without the label of good or bad, you will become perfect, as your Father in heaven is perfect, which means God does not judge. God just is. God does not label things as good or bad. The labeling of things as good or bad sustains the illusory sense of *me* as the doer. Witness everything as one big interconnected happening. So remember: have *no knowledge* of what is *good* or *bad*, and you may find yourself back in the garden.

The Self does not speak. Therefore you have to be very quiet to hear it.

Using your intellect to understand that your true nature is like a fish caught in a net. The more the fish struggles, the more it becomes entangled.

"You" and "The Universe" rise and fall simultaneously. They are One. Your true nature is prior to it.

The Universe is
A big, fat illusion,
But not an hallucination.

27
Thoughts
(#1)

When we lovingly bring awareness to the fear in other people, compassion arises in us.

"Purpose" and "there being a reason" are chains that bind us.

Isn't it weird that everywhere you go there's a conscious presence already there?

To be perfect means to not put the labels of good or bad on anything.

Thinking you're a person is just a belief that got picked up along the way. Life is just God-imagining.

The totality of peace can only be found within.

28
One

At your center a marvelous jewel,
No need for a shovel or any tool
A marvelous journey that didn't happen
Your mind, it slowly starts a snappin'.
Welcome home. I've never left.
I am gone, the biggest theft.
Release me from your grip
Careful now, don't you slip.

My hands are shaking, I'm starting to sweat.
My heart is beating. If I had to bet
I'd say I'm dying, or was I ever born?
How can I find something that isn't lost?
What's left that hasn't been tossed?
Where' s the bridge that needs to be crossed?

What's the answer, is there one?
Where's the path, is there one?
Right or wrong, is there one?

One

29
Surrender
(#3)

Oh, God, in your infinite oneness,
    I surrender to thee, for I am an empty shell,
A small vessel to be used for your love to flow
through,
    Extending to everyone and everything.

Use me as you will to do good or bad,
Right or wrong or any other thing
The situation commands,
For I am but a humble servant.
Take from me what you want,
Give to me what you will,
For my opinions have been extinguished.
I will be as a blind child,
Only seeing you in every act,
In every deed.

If I am meant to protect the weak,
Then let me protect them with every cell of my being.

If I am meant to give,
Then allow me to give all I have,
And all that I am,
Down to my last drop of blood.

If I am meant to comfort,
Then allow me to suffer,
So that I can comfort people
From the deepest recess of my heart.

And if I should stray,
Please bring me back to the narrow path,
In any way you see fit.

30
Letter to Mankind

It is all gone for me. I have nothing left. Oh, what a joy it is to be stripped of the anger, the hatred, the rage! I want nothing but to be of service to you. I need just a little bit of food and drink to sustain myself in order to continue to help and serve.

Use me, world, in any way you see fit, for my life is not my own. It is yours. Send to me the weary, so that they may rest. Give to me the angry, so I may swallow the anger and they can have peace. Let the tortured souls find me, so that I may listen and give.

Let me absorb your pain, and together we shall turn it into glory. Allow me to comfort those in need, for my own suffering has been transformed, and I have nothing left but to give back to the scared and the lonely.

God, give them all a gentle, loving nudge so they may open up and allow the healing to begin.

Here I stand, waiting, for the next troubled souls to come my way, so I may carry them until they can stand on their own.

31
The New "Our Father"

Our Source,

Who is in Heaven and outside of it,
Your kingdom has come,
Your will forever done,
Omnipotent and ever-reaching
Give or give not our daily bread,
Choose or choose not to forgive our wrong,
Yet we will forgive those who do wrong to us.
 Test us always with temptation,
And make us aware that the Evil One keeps us
    separate from you,
For yours is the power and the glory forever and ever.

Amen.

32
The Second Coming

It is a belief of many people that after Jesus was crucified he then rose from the dead, hung around for a few weeks, and then took off never to be seen again, but promising to come back—the occasion to be known as the second coming of Christ. It is my opinion that after he suffered and then died on the cross, he was buried in a mass grave next to the hill on which he was crucified, which historically was done with "criminals" by the Romans in that area of the world, at that time.

Once your true nature is known, you will see that this canonical resurrection story is irrelevant to understanding, and it is only the ego that wants to perpetuate itself, play God, and keep living on forever. It was years after Christ's death before that story was concocted. Historically, the first fragments of any of the gospels in the New Testament we have are from around 150 A.D. That is more than 110 years after Jesus died. Then 150 years after that we have full length or complete gospels that eventually made it into the New Testament. That's a lot of years for a lot of egos to re-write their version of the story, taking out or adding to the gospels that were written a century after Jesus' death.

Historically it is known, with no argument from scholars, that Matthew and John were actual disciples of Christ, but that Mark and Luke never even met Christ. Enlightenment, or the Kingdom of Heaven, is sometimes referred to as Christ consciousness. The second coming, or resurrection, is when Christ consciousness arises through you. What I mean is that when the revelation of the unicity and totality of God arises through a body-mind organism, this is the second coming of Christ. When the same understanding that arose through Christ happens through any body-mind organism, this is called Christ consciousness, entering the Kingdom of Heaven, God-realization, enlightenment or whatever words you want to use to point to this revelation.

33
Free Will

"I form the light and create darkness.
I make peace and create evil."
—Isaiah 45:7

Most people will tell you God is good and the devil is bad. Most people say God has a plan. Almost everyone will tell you that you have free will. When you think yourself to be a separate person, you live through the eyes of dichotomy. Once the idea that I am an individual doer in control and having free will is there, it is common to look at God as an individual, separate entity who is usually good; then, of course, we must find God a counterpart, which is—the devil, or Satan, who is bad. This is what I call having a split mind. It is the classic story of good vs. evil, which has been around for millennia. This is the way most people see it, and the way they live their lives. Everything is labeled as good or bad, depending upon their opinion of whatever situation occurs, and that's where all the trouble begins.

When we see God as having human attributes, we are bringing God down to the level of a person. We are then boxing in, limiting and trying to know God with our minds. This has been tried for thousands of years. Think of all the wars fought "in God's name" or believing God is on whomever's side; the results have been disastrous. This is only one of the problems with seeing God as an entity.

Another problem that happens with this line of thinking is that the logical person is going to start to question God's motives for all the pain and suffering, death and destruction that happens in the world. Luckily we can then blame the devil for all the "bad stuff." But then why does God allow the devil to do all this "bad stuff"? On the other hand, how are we to know what's really good or bad?

Let's say a nine-year-old girl loses her mother to cancer. The year is 1912. Sounds pretty bad, Right? But then that girl works day and night for 30 years and comes up with a cure for cancer in the year 1942. So what looked bad at first has now become a "good" thing. Because cancer is a major killer of people all over the world, all the people who would have died from 1942 to, let's say 2013, would have lived. That's a lot of people worldwide. With this new scenario, many of those "saved" people who would have died now have lived long lives and had lots of kids. Those kids who never would have been born would now have grown up and had kids of their own, and those kids would have grown up and had more kids. So by the year 2013, there are hundreds of millions, if not a billion more people in the world, thus creating a major food shortage in which many people suffer and die, with some of the starving now turning to crime and violence to feed themselves and their families. This would be considered bad ... all because that little girl grew up to find a cure for cancer.

My point of all this babbling—in a simplistic example, to be sure—is that with the split mind, God being good and the devil being bad, it leaves us feeling empty and confused. We still don't have an answer to why God would either let this happen or allow the devil to make so much trouble. It would be bad enough if we all believed in just *one* separate God, but it gets worse with all the different groups of people believing in different gods, adding to all the trouble like prejudice, hate, fear, war, ignorance of other people's beliefs and so on, pitting people against one another, each group believing that "their god" is the correct one and the other group of people are wrong and vice versa. The belief in God as an entity that is separate from us has caused immeasurable pain and suffering among us, as the past and present have clearly shown.

But what about the future? Are we to go with those beliefs, hoping things are just going to get better? They will not, because no matter how much tolerance we have for each others' beliefs about our separate entity gods, at the end of the day, whoever believes whatever he believes, tolerance goes only so far, and there is still the thought uppermost: *my* group is right and *your* group is wrong. That's because one's very identity is dependent on that religious belief, and as long as that belief is there, nothing will ever change.

The answer is that if the identity is seen as illusory, we stop seeing God as having an identity. Then we get rid of the idea of the "bad devil," by knowing that everything is God and everything is one. Since God is now *not* an entity, separate from manifestation, but is everything in as well as the source of manifestation itself, there is no *me* here anymore, there are no questions to ask God, as potential, manifests into every different form in the universe, just to experience itself! Since God is not an entity and there is no *me* here, everything is now seen as a random happening, so there is no one to blame for anything, and there is no *me* here to do the blaming.

This understanding takes away the emptiness and confusion. It also does something better than getting answer after answer to question after question, for it alleviates the need for any more questions at all. So God is no longer under its own spell of divine hypnosis, thinking that it is a person, but realizes its own divinity through the person, the organism, blissful peace and contentment, and fearlessness running through it, for all the answers have been answered because all the questioning stops. This brings contentment to life that is indescribable. God is omnipresent, which means present in all places at the same time.

Another way to say it is: God just is. God is not a person, nor does God have human-like qualities. This idea is just an anthropomorphic hallucination created by the mind that God is like a person. Even the word God is incorrect in that by calling the unnamable God, we are giving God an identity, an identity that is separate from our identity, which is an illusion. If you think yourself to be self conscious and created, it is only natural that the mind would then seek to find a creator. But *you* have not been created, for all of this is just an appearance that manifests out of potential into consciousness. Free will is a nasty little idea formed in the darkest recesses of the mind, which in turn causes nothing but suffering, pain, separation from God, confusion, ignorance and judgment of one another. True understanding of God does not come in a thought or mental construct. To know God you can only say, "God is unknowable." That is the only way to know God. So it is God who is writing this book. God who is reading it. God who has awakened and realized itself through some organisms and God who has *not* awakened and is still dreaming through other organisms. As I said, it's all God. By the way, it was God who said that, too.

34
Thoughts
(#2)

The source of everything is less than one!

Just as sweetness and sugar cannot be separate from one another, you can and have never been separate from yourself, which is the unmanifested source of everything.

If a woman bathing herself in sunlight on a secluded beach were to fall asleep, when she woke up she would be the awakener and the one who had awakened.

Consciousness is one. The source of consciousness is prior to one. It is truly unnamable, although I shall point to that by saying it is potential. It is a true enigma that cannot be known by the intellect. Yet through constant repetition of thinking with the intellect, suddenly the mind opens up and then a non-conceptual understanding appears, not out of nowhere but in a way as though the clouds parted and revealed the sun, which has always been there, no matter whether you were aware of it.

35
Who's in Charge?
(Spontaneous and Random)

Your destiny is not your destiny, until it is your destiny! What does this mean? It means there is no pre-destiny, but once an event happens, it couldn't have happened any other way.

God is not a person. God does not have a plan and does not make decisions. God is everything; everything is not created by a person-like God that is separate from its creation, but everything is literally made out of God. In other words the ingredients that make up everything is God.

Although all words are feeble in the attempt to describe God, one word that I use to point to that which is unnamable is *potential*—what things are before they become things. So God in its rawest form is the potential of all things, and this potential manifests, quite spontaneously, into the actual physicality of everything. Then there is the person, who is like an antenna receiving information from everything else; but the person is not in charge, either. Everything moves and acts connected with everything else. It all just rolls along with billions of unforeseen variables playing off each other. Decisions are not decided; they happen according to whatever variables come into play.

With human beings there is a strange sense of separateness which leads to a belief in being a doer. This belief leads to the idea of free will, and then all is lost. Seeing that it is just a belief, nothing is ever really lost. Surrender the idea of being a person having free will. Give it up to the potential or source of all things, and when the idea of being a person who is in charge leaves, the organism then reverts back to its true nature, and with it comes a relief and peace that truly has no opposite. It takes a certain amount of time—let's say a hundredth of a second—for a thought to appear out of nowhere; then there is awareness of that thought; then there is comprehension of what the thought means, so by the time you comprehend the thought it is in the past! There is no doer and there is no thinker. All is God and God just *is*.

36
The Ultimate Goal

A love for you that has no equal,
The second coming a profound sequel.
The kingdom has come; it is among you.
It is all yours; that's who it belongs to.

In the wind, the rain and the stars above,
Forever present, your unconditional love.
How can I thank you, the glorious source?
For some the illusion must run its course.

To be of service, it is my reward.
Let me guide them further toward
The ultimate goal. It starts with forgiveness.
May I help on this path, the path to deliverance?

So use me, use me, use me up
As much as you'd like, please fill my cup.
Whether white as snow or black as coal
Service to mankind is the ultimate goal.

37
And Yet Still More
Things I Have Learned
(#3)

- The laughter of my three-year-old niece gives me one of the greatest feelings I have ever had!

- One's level of emotional stability and maturity will attract the like.

- I can let go and watch life flow.

- Everything in life happens quite spontaneously without there being a "doer" anywhere.

* The universe is completely connected, plays a part in every single event anywhere, and free will is an illusion. The illusionary idea of free will allows the ego to believe it can pretend it is God.

- It is impossible to ever "win" an argument, because when you show someone he is wrong using anger, everybody loses.

  That is why I have learned it is better to be happy and make peace with people than to dominate them and be "right."

- Kindness can spread through people like wildfire.

- Resentment is like swallowing poison and waiting for the other person to die.

- Gossip can be deadly.

- What you put out into the universe finds its way back to you.

- You can't help people who don't want to change and aren't ready to receive that help.

- *All* emotional wounds can be mended through the magic of forgiveness.

- Every selfless act seems to bring me two steps closer to God, and every selfish act seems to bring me one step away from God.

- There are many things in this world I would die for, but almost nothing I would kill for.

- Intimacy can be better than sex.

- Many elderly people are very lonely.

- Three of the most important things every person on the planet wants is to be heard, loved and validated.

- When it comes to happiness, you have to give it away in order to keep it.

- Spirituality is better when you take the religion out of it.

- Love *is* the answer.

- All the big spiritual teachers are pointing to the same thing, which in the end is complete and total surrender to God.

- Attachment to anything leads to suffering, but the solution is to look at all you posses as if it were just borrowed.

- It is difficult for the world to live as one with the belief in different gods that are seen as entities.

- I am not separate from God. This knowledge has brought me through to an indescribable peace.

- Every woman kisses just a little bit differently, and whatever woman I am with, when she reads this sentence, will know she kisses the best.

- Dealing with and feeling my feelings really isn't that scary.

- Complaining is detrimental to the happiness of you and everyone around you.

- It is better to find a solution than to complain about a problem.

- A simple smile can have profound effects on people.

- Most of the time it is better to listen than to talk.

- Time and space have come suddenly and will leave quickly.

- I can be kind and let the universe worry about the rest.

- Almost every person who gains power fears losing it.

- Every great empire will eventually fall.

- To have deep spiritual wisdom you must first unlearn what you have learned.

- There is knowledge beyond conceptual understanding.

38
Heaven, Hell, Rebirth

Over the millennia there have been many stories told about what happens to *you* after the body dies. One very popular story that has been infiltrating its way into Western society is rebirth. It seems that more and more people have given up the idea that you have only one shot at life and either end up in heaven or hell. With rebirth you get to come back over and over again until you "get it right," whatever that means.

Birth, Rebirth
The major problem with this idea is the assumption that you have been born in the first place. If you focus your awareness on this birth, you'll find that *you* have never been born, not once, not ever—that it is only the body that has been born, and with it comes a neurological connection that makes it appear there is a separate doer here, making choices with free will. If you thoroughly and courageously investigate this birth, you will see it as false, and the story book fantasies of an "afterlife" will fade away in the same way your childhood belief in Santa Claus faded away as you got older. As a child you believed in Santa Claus, and boy did he seem real; then some new information came in, and the belief just faded away. In the exact same way, the belief that you are a person is there, and then through investigation that belief will just fade away and you will "die" to that old way of thinking and be "reborn" into the glorious understanding of the total unicity of God, understanding that this body is nothing more than a manifested extension of the imperishable source of all things.

"Do not conform yourselves to the standards of this world, but let God transform you inwardly by a complete change of your mind." —Romans 12:2

Only something separate from the whole would believe it has been born and will die, and there is nothing separate from the whole. Your true nature is the "unborn" or "pre-born," pure awareness. It manifests spontaneously into active consciousness, which arises out of pure awareness, or another word I use to point is potentiality. I shall give you a few more examples.

Zero plus zero equals zero. If I were to hold out my hand and there was nothing in it, and I said, "Double what is in my hand," what would your answer be? Obviously, it would be, "Nothing." Another example would be that you couldn't have re-fried beans if there were no such things as beans.

Finally an example I think is even more potent is this: let's say you and I go to the movie theater to see a film. There we are with our popcorn and soda and milk duds. As we are witnessing the movie being played, we both go through an array of different emotions. We may laugh or cry. We may feel sad or angry. We may get scared half to death and be jolted in our seats, causing us to spill $20 worth of popcorn all over the place. Finally the movie is over and the credits start to roll. As the theater begins to empty we stay in our seats still drinking in the movie we just witnessed.

I turn to you and say, "No one really knows what happens to those people on the screen or where they go once the movie is over."

After giving me a strange look you say something like, "Those people weren't really there. They just seemed to be there. They were really made of light that condensed down to give the appearance of being real. How can they go anywhere once the movie is over if they weren't really there in the first place?"

"But I saw and heard them, and I laughed and cried, and I was scared! What do you mean they weren't real?" I argue.

In your loving kindness you explain to me again that it was just an illusion made out of light. The screen was real and unchanging, but the pictures came and went and had no real substance of their own.

Without the screen we wouldn't have seen the pictures, yet the screen had no opinion about what pictures made of light might have danced upon it. It was the light of the projector that brought the pictures to life on the unchanging background of the screen.

So it is with life. The screen is the absolute. The light of the projector is the consciousness, and the pictures created are the universe. Without a screen the light and the pictures are meaningless, which means the light and the pictures it creates are dependent on the screen. While the screen is completely indifferent to what is shown on it, without a screen, nothing can be seen. So to know what happens after this "life" is over, you need to know the beginning. This is why Jesus said to his disciples in the Gospel of Thomas, saying #18, when they had asked about how their end would be. He said, "Have you discovered the beginning, then, so that you are seeking the end? For where the beginning is the end be. Blessed is the one who stands at the beginning: That one will know the end and will not taste death."

"What Jesus meant by this statement was that your "beginning" is the source. The source is prior to time and space, prior to birth and death, prior to the universe and also prior to consciousness. Only that which has no beginning can have no end, and this is what he meant by saying you have eternal life. Everything that has a beginning has an end. So he did not mean that when a body dies some *you* goes on and lives for eternity in a forward, linear fashion. He means because your true nature is the unborn source, you are eternal because since you truly have no beginning you can never die, because you have never been born in the first place. This is because potential is eternal.

Heaven, Hell and the "Evil One"

Satan, the devil or the evil one conjures up all sorts of medieval imagery of some horned, goat-like being with fire and sulfur and pitchfork. Let us finally put that to rest once and for all, because it does nobody any good except the religious organizations who profit from your fear as they make up story after story of some place "down there" that you will go to after you "die" that will be terrible and horrible and beyond belief. It is a ridiculous notion and only creates chaos and fear and ignorance while lining the pockets of rich, greedy people who want to scare you into submission and get rich doing it. They have done a pretty good job of it for 1500 years, and it is up to us to stop it and to not allow it to continue one more generation. Let it end now!

Stop believing it, and it will go away just like a terrible nightmare ends upon waking up. The "Evil One" that Jesus refers to many times in the Bible is nothing more than the ego, or sense of separate doership. He warns again and again to be aware of this idea of free will as he repeatedly tells you about believing that everything is God.

The "Evil One" is what will keep you in hell, for hell is nothing more than separation from God. If the belief of being a separate person is there, there can be no full surrendering of this ego to God. When that surrendering has been accomplished, you have entered the Kingdom of Heaven.

So let's review: the devil is the ego. Hell is when the ego appears real and creates the illusion of being separate from God, which is the definition of hell. Heaven is when the identity of the person is dissolved, moving you out of hell and entering you into the Kingdom of Heaven. When you surrender to God your idea of free will, the seeker is evaporated and the true unicity of everything is understood. The Kingdom of Heaven is now upon you.

Have you ever stopped for a moment and really looked at the idea of what most people say about heaven? This is the most common story I have heard: When a "good" person dies, the individual soul goes off to a place (even though Jesus tells us in Luke 17:21 that it is *not* a place where you live for eternity having every wish and desire granted and fulfilled forever and ever and ever). What's wrong with this picture? Well, many things.

The first thing wrong with it is that here on earth the "good" is only good because of the bad—meaning it is the dichotomy of good and bad, or the comparison of good with bad that makes things good or bad.

What I am saying is that a cold beer at the end of a long, hard day's work tastes so good because you just toiled and worked and sweated and suffered all day, which wasn't too much fun, and so at the end of the day, in comparison to the long, tough day, the beer tastes good. By the way, I don't advocate drinking; do whatever you feel like doing. I'm just using it as an example.

Or how about this: if we lived forever and every baby was always born in perfect health, would your child being born still be an incredible life-altering experience? It is the relation between good and bad that makes the good, so good. If when we were born we could all immediately walk perfectly, would seeing your baby take its first steps mean anything to you anymore? I'm sure you can come up with a hundred more examples on your own.

Another thing that is wrong is the childish, selfish, greedy, disgusting idea that in heaven you get whatever you want, as much as you want, whenever you want. If that's not the epitome of egotism, I don't know what is. The place called heaven is nothing more than a spoiled child's dream world. And man, do the churches do a good job selling it. There seem to be billions lined up to buy it. A measly 80 or so years on earth, and you get all that just for saying, "I believe in Jesus"?

It is time to wake up and understand that the peace of God doesn't come that easily. That's why Jesus had a teaching. Even after years of sitting with Jesus on a daily basis, living with him, looking into his eyes and hearing the words coming directly out of his mouth, his disciples still did not understand him. Why do you think he spoke in parables? Because what he was saying was the deepest of the deep and couldn't be understood with a few sentences received by the mind. If the churches were right about heaven being a place, the New Testament should be one sentence long: "Believe in me and go to a place called heaven and get whatever you want forever." The end.

Yet it is not one sentence long. It is filled with a deep, profound teaching that transforms the person into a servant of God, not a spoiled child who gets everything it wants. So know that embarking on the true, spiritual path is not for the weak hearted. It is the greatest, most amazing roller coaster ride of adventure and self-discovery that the mind could ever conjure. That's why it cannot be understood with the mind but must be known from the deepest depths of your being, with a true, transforming revelation that can come only from within, that evaporates the seeker and leaves you with nothing ... nothing but God.

39
A Daily Occurrence

We cannot find the underlying unicity of all things by seeking it from the point of view of a separate person, yet ironically that is how the journey begins. For in the seeking, the very seeker itself melts away, revealing the unicity that has always been there when potential finds itself, which then brings peace to the organism.

Ah, but alas! We do not become superhuman. We still feel in the same way, if not even more intensely. We still can feel some anger, pain and sadness, although those emotions don't seem to stick to us in the same way they used to. In my experience—and I used to be very angry a lot of the time—when anger does rarely occur now it seems to blow through me like a breeze and very quickly goes away. Once full understanding is there, it does not leave and does not change, although because the body is still there it is going to still have thoughts, memories and feelings of all kinds.. There is something that is remarkably different about it that I just can't explain.

The understanding just seems to "turn down the dial," so to speak, on all of my "negative" emotions, thoughts and feelings. There is no longer a feeling of being trapped in them. They come, they go, and that's it. The slate has been wiped clean and now everything just moves right through me so quickly. (Maybe it's the prune juice I've been drinking. Just kidding.) All of my practices have now become effortless and just seem to be there waiting to be used in whatever situation comes up. When I say "used," I mean a certain situation comes up, followed by a thought or emotion, then a resolution and it all floats away.

What is different or missing is this idea that it just happened to a *me*. That is totally gone, and it is beautiful. There is just a witnessing of it all happening spontaneously. There isn't an inner involvement in it anymore, although on the outside, or to another person looking, it appears the same way it always has. But on the inside it is now seen as just a long string of fluid happenings, one event occurring after the other in a beautiful, harmonious dance of life, or God just experiencing itself.

40
You Are God

You are God; you are what is. Because you *are* prior to oneness, you are unable to be aware of yourself. In order to know yourself, you have to split yourself into separateness, or twoness. Thus you manifest the feeling "I AM," which is the birth of dichotomy, in order to experience yourself.

Now, the spell of divine hypnosis of separateness is so strong that the body can live for eighty years without there being any realization of one's true nature. One way for you to "realize" your spaciousness is to continuously ask yourself the questions:

Who am I?
What am I?
Do I have form?
Was "I" really born?

www.ingramcontent.com/pod-product-compliance
Lightning Source LLC
Chambersburg PA
CBHW060542100426
42742CB00013B/2417